getting a **TOP JOB**
... (IT)

For my father, Robert

THE TIMES

getting a **TOP JOB** in ... IT

david yardley

KOGAN PAGE

First published in 2001

Kogan Page Limited
120 Pentonville Road
London N1 9JN

The views expressed in this book are those of the author, and are not necessarily
the same as those of Times Newspapers Ltd.

British Library Cataloguing in Publication Data

A CIP record for this book is available from the British Library.

ISBN 0 7494 3556 9

Typeset by Saxon Graphics Ltd, Derby
Printed and bound in Great Britain by Clays Ltd, St Ives plc

Contents

Acknowledgements

For granting permission to reprint copyright material, I would like to thank *Computer Weekly*. Information regarding careers within Government Communications Headquarters (GCHQ) is protected by Crown Copyright and is reproduced with permission. I would also like to thank the following organisations who gave up a lot of their precious time to answer the questions I had prepared for them:

IBM UK	Pearson Publishing
Intel Ireland	Eidos
Oracle	Cisco Systems
The Post Office	GCHQ
British Telecom	

Finally, I would like to thank my wife, Anne, for her unwavering commitment in editing and proof-reading my typescript; a true professional.

Introduction

Steve Ballmer, the billionaire president of Microsoft, has told world business leaders that the real revolution on the Internet is only just beginning, with the creation of the virtual marketplace via online commerce.

According to Mr Ballmer... Internet services will allow manufacturers, suppliers, dealers and consumers to conduct business with almost 100 per cent efficiency on the Internet.

The Times, *October 13, 1999*

The impact of computing and IT

There can be few people today who have not witnessed the dramatic impact IT has had on our lives. No longer do we only use IT within science and industry; we now use IT for our own entertainment and development as well. This is great news for anyone wanting a top job in IT. Today's IT industry is an exciting place to work – the number of opportunities available continues to rise and average salaries remain high compared to other jobs. Despite a small decrease in vacancies during the latter part of 1999, the industry is still experiencing a skills shortage – there are not enough *skilled* people to satisfy the constant demands of businesses eager to harness the power of IT and the Internet.

Recent research has also shown that employers have started, once more, to hire significant numbers of graduates to fill their IT and e-commerce vacancies. During 1999, the number of graduates entering the profession rose by an estimated 50 per cent to around 5,000 graduates. This number represents the largest increase in graduate recruitment for over a decade.

1

Over the next few years, industry experts expect the number of graduates entering the profession to grow just as rapidly as the demand for Internet and e-commerce skills increases. However, there is still a long way to go before companies reach the levels of graduate recruitment they achieved during the 1980s and early 1990s. Even now, the proportion of graduates entering the IT profession is still way below the proportion many experts believe is necessary to keep pace with demand. It is expected that the majority of graduates moving into IT this year will go directly into e-commerce positions rather than traditional IT posts.

Organisations recruiting IT staff no longer seek 'technophiles' who are self-taught 'geeks'. They require skilled 'all-rounders' who can understand and enhance the businesses they support. Don't be misled into thinking the only people capable of attracting a top job in IT are computer science graduates. As you'll discover later within this book, many of the top employers in the UK actually prefer *non-IT* graduates; yes, even those from arts and classical disciplines. A desire to learn IT skills coupled with strong interpersonal skills is more than good enough to work within the IT profession.

Many organisations that recruit IT staff have at last realised that a degree is only the starting point of a successful career. Experience counts for a lot in the IT world and your ability to market your experience will to some extent determine how well you progress in your 'top' job. Similarly, top jobs in IT are no longer exclusive to new graduates. Experienced business people are now finding their commercial skills and experience pay handsomely, especially if they possess IT-related postgraduate qualifications.

IT seeks to meet the demands of business wherever that might be, and if you are to be successful, you must be able to relate IT capability to business needs. If you can do this, as some of the business people identified in the industry case studies within the book have done, then you too will achieve success.

There is now no better time to get a top job in IT. Not only do computing and IT enjoy a high profile in the media; universities and major employers are now working together to train graduates and postgraduates for successful and long-term careers within the IT profession. Even the UK government is now endorsing the new 'Internet age' by trying to adopt a pan-European approach to help businesses develop using the Internet.

Similarly, there are now many more opportunities for existing graduates and postgraduates to change careers and move into the IT profession. As you will discover from the many case studies within this book, many successful IT professionals did not originally plan a career in IT – they were already enjoying successful careers in other professions.

If _you_ want a top job in IT, then you should congratulate yourself on having already taken the first (and most important!) step – by reading this book. It will give you an up-to-date insight into the IT industry, how it has developed into the lucrative and rewarding industry it is today and how you can find a top job within it.

But what is a top job? The IT industry is now seen as a 'cool' place to work – but it has earned that tag for some very serious reasons:

- Salaries are high compared to other industries.
- With demand for skilled IT staff, IT companies offer many benefits to attract and keep staff.
- European and even worldwide travel is possible (often on a regular basis).
- IT is a global industry. You can use your IT skills in just about any major city throughout the world.
- If you can be in 'the right place at the right time', especially regarding new Internet start-up companies, you can move up the career ladder very quickly, picking up lucrative share options along the way.

If you are an IT graduate, or a graduate in a non-IT (and non-numerate) discipline, this book will help you find a top job in IT. The book will describe the nature of the IT industry and the main areas within which you can work. For established professionals seeking a career move in IT, this book can help.

Top jobs in IT

Computing and IT are now used in just about every walk of life, from the demanding worlds of science, medicine, defence, politics and business to the more relaxing pastimes of recreation, entertainment and personal development. Figure 0.1 shows where and how computing and IT can be used – it is by no means the

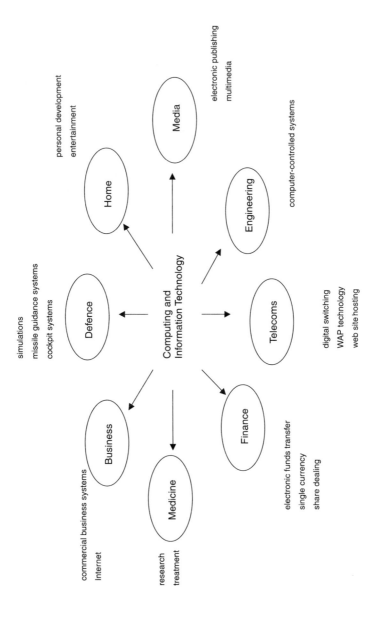

Figure 0.1 The many uses of computing and IT

complete picture, but it should help in deciding your route into finding a top job within IT.

Included in the book will be a number of company profiles, which will examine some of the major employers within the industry and case studies of their employees. These case studies identify the roles and responsibilities of many top IT professionals, how they got there and what you need to do if you want to work in a similar role.

This book can only provide a general guide to the many opportunities available for training and employment within the IT industry. If you follow the advice within it, however, you will be able to use your time well in planning a rewarding career in IT. Whatever you plan to do, be confident – plan for success!

1 *Top IT skills and the IT shortage*

There have always been skills shortages in IT and there have always been people who complain they cannot get a job. Whilst this is probably true for all professions, the IT profession *is* different. IT is changing at an alarmingly fast rate, and just as the traditional craftsman had to change to keep up with the times, so too must today's IT professional. The $64,000 question is of course: what skills do I need for a top job in IT?

A good place to start would be to review the SSP (salary survey publication) surveys published in conjunction with *Computer Weekly*. These appear regularly within *Computer Weekly* and are one of the key indicators used by IT employers and recruitment agencies. These surveys analyse the advertisements for computer professionals in the trade press and quality national newspapers – take them seriously, they are a true reflection of what is happening within the industry. The survey analysing trends during April–June 2000 (2Q00) provides startling proof – if any were needed – of the pace of change within the IT industry (see Table 1.1).

Six new entrants appeared in the top 25 skills, three of which – XML (Extensible Markup Language), CORBA (Common Object Request Broker) and WAP (Wireless Application Protocol) – did not even appear at all a year ago. One of the others, Solaris, appears in the top 25 for the first time and the other two, Ada and Delphi, have been in and out of the rankings regularly over the last few years. What is probably even more incredible is that these six new entrants have displaced some fairly strong competition: Novell, RPG400, SAP, Lotus Notes, MVS (Multiple Virtual Storage) and DB2.

The survey clearly indicates that Internet-related skills are rapidly overtaking the more established application development skills. No longer is Windows NT development the

Table 1.1   IT skills most in demand

Position 2Q00	Position 2Q99	Skill	Jobs on Offer		Change Q200 v Q299
			in 2Q00	in 2Q99	
1	3	C++	4,401	6,849	−36%
2	10	Java	4,088	2,410	+70%
3	21	Internet	3,431	1,149	+199%
4	4	Unix	3,208	6,137	−48%
5	2	Windows NT	2,868	7,277	−61%
6	1	Oracle	2,616	7,295	−64%
7	6	SQL	2,563	5,069	−49%
8	5	Visual Basic	2,362	5,070	−53%
9	7	C	2,313	4,621	−50%
10	25	HTML	2,077	982	+112%
11	17	TCP/IP	1,169	1,374	−15%
12	new entry	XML	934	0	n/a
13	23	Object-oriented	912	1,123	−19%
14	new entry	CORBA	727	0	n/a
15	24	LAN	624	1,096	−43%
16	9	Windows	622	2,921	−79%
17	26	WAN	606	961	−37%
18	41	Solaris	518	332	+56%
19	12	Sybase	494	1,675	−71%
20	45	Ada	402	280	+44%
21	29	Delphi	396	784	−49%
22	23	Progress	381	645	−41%
23	19	Access	377	1,198	−69%
24	8	Cobol	351	2,930	−88%
25	new entry	WAP	346	0	n/a
all jobs			25,276	46,916	−46%

(Source: SSP/_Computer Weekly_ Quarterly Survey of Appointments Data and Trends)

main priority – this has been captured by Java and Internet development.

Probably the most important trend in the survey is the continued rise in Java, now second in the table behind C++. During April, May and June, over 4,000 jobs specified Java skills, 70 per cent more than the same period in 1999.

Incredibly, demand for generic Internet skills has increased even more rapidly than demand for Java; during this period it rose by three times the previous year's level. As a result, it has moved up 18 places in the table to lie just behind Java.

The final member of the Internet skills trio, HTML (Hypertext Markup Language) has also been popular, with demand running at double that of 1999. HTML was specified in more than 2,000 job advertisements. Demand for XML skills is also high, with 900 jobs specifying it as a requirement, pushing XML into twelfth position in the table. Much of this demand has been as a result of the software houses and IT consultancies embarking on more and more e-commerce and Internet-related projects. If you are looking for a top job in Internet development, these two employment sectors are likely to offer the best opportunities – software houses accounted for just under two-thirds of all Java jobs on offer, and over two-thirds of all HTML and XML jobs.

Another key skill fundamental to the majority of networked IT systems is Transmission Control Protocol/Internet Protocol (TCP/IP). This still remains in demand although the level of demand has dropped nearly 15 per cent since 1999. This should not be a worry; TCP/IP and other key networking protocols still underpin just about every major IT system, which is why it has risen six places in the skills ranking.

Whilst the opinion of many professionals within the industry confirms the reports that the Internet is the future of business and IT, what is surprising is that the number of Internet-related jobs has rocketed in a climate of declining numbers of jobs in the IT market generally. IT recruitment continued to fall in the second quarter of 2000, for the sixth consecutive quarter. The total number of jobs advertised was a little over 25,000, down by almost half on the same period last year. This sharp fall in demand is hardly surprising considering the massive number of jobs advertised for year 2000 projects all over the UK. Now in the relatively calm and stable post-year 2000 development environment, recruitment targets are slowly returning to levels of previous years.

The skills shortage, however encouraging for anyone wanting a top job in IT, must be treated with a small dose of caution. A recruitment manager, asked recently what the hot skills in IT were, responded by saying 'Java, java, java', he was obviously trying to capture the overall picture for future IT development as briefly as possible, but nothing in life is ever that simple. Commercial experience of Java and C++ *is* very useful if you want a successful career as an application developer, especially if you have been using them in the banking and finance sectors for a few years. Having recruited staff for my own company at some of the major annual recruitment fairs, I can appreciate the recruitment agent's comments. Many people I speak to, graduates, postgraduates and experienced professionals alike, claim to have Java skills, but have not used them commercially. Those who have are few and far between and usually find top jobs either through being approached by headhunters or through networking colleagues and associates in other companies.

If getting a top job in IT was as simple as reading a book on Java and writing a few programs on your PC at home, we'd all be doing it! The most likely route into a career programming in Java is probably through a degree in an IT-related subject. If you can leave university with Java skills, maybe having completed a Java development project on your 'sandwich' year, you can expect to earn at least £20,000 a year.

Java – the language of the Web

Java is famous for being the language of the Web, and rightly so. Early Java applications were aimed at small Web-based applications or applets, but with Microsoft and HTML dominating the client-side, attention has now focused on server-based applications. IBM is already positioning Java as the server language of the future.

Java owes its existence to James Gosling, a programmer working for Sun, who in 1990 was trying to find a way of developing C++ programs that would run on the widest variety of computer platforms without the need to recompile the program.

The language he developed he called Oak (after the view from his window), but on finding the name already registered, renamed it Java. What he created has now taken the IT world and the Internet development market by storm. According to a Gartner Group survey carried out in 1999, out of 500 IT managers, over 75 per cent were either evaluating, using or planning to use Java.

Java is, of course, a popular and powerful language for one reason; it is portable in the true sense of the word. Any platform that has a Java Virtual Machine (JVM) – the run-time environment that interprets the compiled Java code and performs the required actions – should, in theory, be able to run any Java program.

If you want to become a Java programmer, a good knowledge of C++ will help (most commercial Java programmers come from a C++ background). If you do not possess C programming skills, there are courses available that will help (see Chapter 12), but remember, Java is a complex programming language and not necessarily the ideal choice for an introduction to programming.

Whilst Java is clearly dominating the Internet development market, the competition is increasing and it is worth keeping a close eye on events in the popular IT magazines. For instance, keep an eye on Microsoft's latest object-oriented programming language, C# (pronounced C sharp). It has been launched with the Internet firmly in mind, with the intention that it will be (to a certain extent) a Java-killer. Only time will tell – in the meantime have a look at Microsoft's Web site on the subject: http://msdn.microsoft.com/vstudio/nextgen/technology/csharpintro.asp.

Internet-based application programming languages are not the only Internet-related skills in demand. Tools to design and build commercial Web sites are heavily used now by more and more companies, pushing demand up for skills such as Macromedia Dreamweaver, Shockwave (also from Macromedia) and Allaire ColdFusion.

Exploiting the skills shortage

In *Skills 99*, a report presented to the Department for Education and Employment, two key concerns were raised about the IT industry: the lack of skills in IT professionals and the lack of IT professionals. The first concern represented the *skills gap*, which can be tackled through better training and planning; the latter represented the true skills shortage, that is, the actual *lack of people*. A similar report, commissioned by Microsoft in association with the CSSA (Computer Services and Software Association) and the ITNTO (National Training Organisation for IT), concluded that 75 per cent of the people questioned thought there was an IT skills shortage, a figure that rose to 90 per cent for those working in the finance sector.

Although the number of people in the IT profession has increased by 10 per cent in the last few years, the number of people with the _right_ skills for the job is falling. For anyone wanting to find a top job in IT, this does offer some hope – if you can obtain the right skills for the jobs most in demand, you will have a much better chance of gaining employment. Windows 2000, for instance, is receiving particularly good reviews from IT and business professionals. As more and more IT departments adopt Windows 2000 as their preferred operating system, it could spark off a new generation of specialised IT jobs, transforming the way many IT departments are organised and managed. Currently many IT departments are organised in a fairly traditional way (see Figure 1.1), but this could change to cope with new developments in technology.

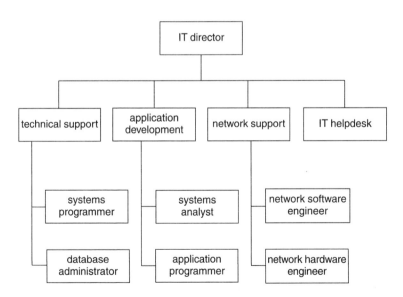

Figure 1.1 The structure of a typical IT department

According to many IT experts, future IT departments will recruit greater numbers of IT development and administration staff, each specialising in a specific aspect of the new operating system. Key system functionality such as security and encryption services and system administration will be where many new jobs are advertised, exploiting the advantages of the new operating system. Compared to Windows NT, Windows 2000 dwarfs its predecessor, both in terms of complexity and capability. Such large-scale announcements are closely watched by the many IT groups representing IT professionals and users alike.

The deployment of Windows 2000 is being taken very seriously by the IT world, and as you are planning to find your perfect job within it, you should take it seriously too. For instance, Dave Race, director of ICL's Windows 2000 programme, has already stated they hope to train 2000 staff in the new operating system by 2001. A leading IT trainer has also predicted there will be a change of job roles with the advent of Windows 2000. With the Windows NT operating system, now firmly established in many organisations, the systems administrator performed all the systems tasks required, from configuring TCP/IP connectivity to ensuring appropriate levels of security and encryption were established and monitored.

Flexibility is the key to a successful career in IT however. The IT industry *is* changing and so is the way IT is used within business. If you want to enter the IT profession and enjoy a successful and rewarding career, you will need to be flexible. Experience has shown that the area in which you start your IT career bears little resemblance to the eventual path your career will follow. Of course, the IT profession is concerned (and sometimes obsessed) with technology, but it is very much a *people* industry. Having a flexible attitude to where you work and what you do can often mean the difference between success and failure in your IT career. Whilst there will always be a need for specialists in the industry, if you possess skills that are in demand in more than one industry sector, you should have a fairly secure and rewarding career. Table 1.2 should give you an idea of the main areas within IT where you could work.

Despite a gradual rise in inflation, IT salaries are still above the underlying rate and well above the national average; Table 1.3 should give you a good idea of what sort of salaries to expect in the main job areas within IT. If you are a high-flying graduate with a 2:1

Table 1.2   Breakdown of IT jobs advertised by industry sector

Sector	Jobs in 2Q00	Jobs in 2Q99	Change
computer suppliers	880	882	0%
software houses	10,792	19,279	–44%
communication companies	3,429	3,431	0%
banking/finance	2,163	6,531	–67%
distribution/retail	970	2,491	–61%
media/publishing	529	739	–28%
manufacturing	320	743	–57%
engineering	425	1,013	–58%
utilities/energy	813	44	–76%
public sector	856	875	–2%

(Source: SSP/_Computer Weekly_ Quarterly Survey of Appointments Data and Trends)

degree (or expect to gain one), or have a few years' relevant IT experience, there are many top IT consultancy companies in the southeast of England who are more than willing to pay you over £20,000 to join them. If that wasn't enough, some of the larger consultancies reward the performance of their staff by giving them shares in the company. Of course, it ties you in for a while, but the rewards, both financially and in terms of career development, can be staggering.

Table 1.3   Average IT salaries on offer

Job Title	Average Salary Offered 2Q00	Average Salary Offered 2Q99	Change
management consultant	£70,723	£72,485	–2%
IT manager	£56,970	£54,039	+5%
systems analyst	£28,601	£28,347	+1%
programmer	£24,087	£23,212	+4%
analyst programmer	£27,666	£26,913	+3%
systems developer	£32,300	£31,349	+3%
PC support analyst	£21,993	£23,368	–6%
software engineer	£29,701	£27,862	+7%
network support technician	£23,219	£20,892	+11%
operator	£21,946	£21,112	+4%

(Source: SSP/_Computer Weekly_ Quarterly Survey of Appointments Data and Trends)

Whilst the top job opportunities still remain largely in the south-east of England, Scotland fared best for the third quarter in succession. Whilst most other regions witnessed a fall in jobs of about 50 per cent, jobs north of the border only fell by a quarter, from 1,300 to 1,000 (see Table 1.4).

Table 1.4   Regional demand for IT jobs

Region	Jobs Advertised 2Q00	Jobs Advertised 2Q99	Change
Inner London	4,019	8,178	–51%
Outer London	3,387	6,511	–48%
Southern England	7,451	14,046	–47%
Wales & West	1,972	4,523	–56%
Midlands & East	2,551	4,509	–43%
Northern England	2,653	5,259	–50%
Scotland	1,023	1,363	–25%

(Source: SSP/*Computer Weekly* Quarterly Survey of Appointments Data and Trends)

During 2000, Andersen Consulting, one of the top management and IT consultancy firms, hit the headlines by offering new graduates a £10,000 joining bonus. Whilst their actions will not necessarily guarantee every consultancy will follow their example, to attract the right calibre staff companies will continually have to reinvent their recruitment packages. In the case of Andersen Consulting, providing the means for potential graduate employees to pay off their student debt has obviously worked. If you are not an IT graduate, don't worry; one of their new starters who received a bonus had gained a 2:1 degree in Classics!

Useful Web sites

Java
www.javasoft.com
www.javadesign.com
www.gamelan.com

www.java.sun.com
www.msdn.microsoft.com

Web site design and development
www.macromedia.com/software/dreamweaver
www.macromedia.com/shockwave
www.allaire.com/products/coldfusion

XML
www.xml.com
www.uccc.ie/xml
www.w3.org.xml

2 Working in IT

A brief history of computing and IT

Advances in computing and IT seem to happen at an incredible pace these days. Thanks to the power of computing, advances in medicine, science and industry improve the lives of millions of people every day. IT, without a doubt, has a fantastic future, allowing us to achieve the impossible, but it is nothing new.

The first computers were developed during the 1940s, following years of research both in the UK and United States, and were so large they would fill an entire room. So great was the financial investment required to build these machines, many experts believed only a few dozen computers would *ever* be needed.

The development of the transistor was a key milestone in the history of computing. Whilst still relatively expensive, computers began to take up less room and consume less power. Soon after came the development of the integrated circuit, which allowed thousands of transistors and other electrical components to be 'printed' onto a piece of silicon – the 'silicon chip' as we know it today.

Since the advent of commercial computing in the 1960s, the IT industry has experienced enormous change, both in culture and technology. If you are looking for a top job in the industry, you need to be aware of these changes. For many people, the lure of high salaries has obscured sensible and rational judgement, causing many unnecessary career disappointments. Today's bandwagon is often tomorrow's dodo – if you jump in head first, you are likely to end up being saddled with unmarketable skills in a mundane job rather than gaining new skills in an exciting, dynamic environment. With a bit of thought and planning, however, you can make sure you not only gain a top job in IT, but move on to even greater career opportunities in the future – not just in the UK, but throughout the world.

Understanding the main types of computers

When you start looking for employment within the IT industry, you will soon discover that some jobs are specific to a particular type of computer platform. The main computer platforms you need to be aware of are detailed below.

Super-computers

Often restricted to large-scale research and development work, super-computers are extremely powerful and can process huge amounts of information (such as complex mathematical calculations and simulations) in a relatively short space of time. Being extremely expensive and limited to specific applications, the super-computer market is fairly static, and may wither away completely as smaller, cheaper machines become available.

Mainframe computers

Historically, commercial computing applications were developed on large mainframe computers and, despite the popularity of smaller computer systems, many organisations could not operate without them. The IBM OS/390 range of mainframe computers contains some of the most powerful commercial mainframes that are used by many organisations throughout the UK and worldwide.

Midrange computers

Large business departments often use medium-sized or 'mini-computers', solely for one or two important business systems, such as order-processing and warehousing systems. The IBM AS/400 range is probably the most popular model of midrange computer you will experience today – although they are now so powerful, the top-end AS/400 market is already competing with the low-end mainframe market. Despite the publicity given to the more popular operating systems such as UNIX and NT, there is a huge shortage of AS/400 skills, both in the US and in the UK.

17

Desktop computers

When IBM launched the first PC during August 1981, the most basic system cost almost £1000. Designed mainly for the home user, the price did not even include a monitor or floppy disk drive for storage. Today's desktop PCs now come with a built in CD ROM or DVD drive, huge amounts of disk space, a sound card and stereo speakers, whilst being capable of displaying 16.3 million colours. This is the standard specification of a 'multimedia' PC, its development being driven by people buying computers to play games. In fact, the modern multimedia PC owes much to high-specification PC games such as Tomb Raider, which placed even greater demands on PC hardware.

PCs are now an everyday commodity owing to their enormous versatility and ease of use. Coupled with their low price tag for a relatively high-performance computer, their growth has been unstoppable. With software vendors, such as Microsoft, providing numerous applications for the PC, there seems little doubt that the desktop revolution is here to stay. Microsoft's latest PC operating system, Windows 2000, contains over 30 million lines of code but can be loaded onto a PC from a standard CD. The PC is now so powerful, many organisations are developing applications on it that historically would have required a mainframe or mini-computer. Table 2.1 should give you an indication of just how quickly the PC has progressed in terms of architecture and performance.

Table 2.1   Advances in processor power

Initial Launch Date	Processor	Number of Transistors	Architecture	Max Speed
1/6/1979	8088	29,000	16-bit	8 Mhz
1/2/1982	80286	134,000	16-bit	12.5 Mhz
17/10/1985	80386	275,000	32-bit	33 Mhz
10/4/1989	80486	1.2 million	32-bit	50 Mhz
22/3/1993	Pentium	3.1 million	32-bit	66 Mhz
7/5/1997	Pentium II	7.5 million	32-bit	450 Mhz
26/2/1999	Pentium III	28.1 million	32-bit	1 Ghz
2000	Itanium	320 million	64-bit	800 Mhz

The evolution of computer systems

Mainframe computing

From the earliest days of computing, up until the 1980s, the traditional view of the computer system was based on the 'mainframe' computer. Mainframe computing has been around for decades, which is why it is sometimes (unfairly) called a 'legacy' system. Despite the advance of other technologies, the mainframe still provides an extremely powerful platform on which large, mundane and repetitive processing (batch processing) can occur within a robust and secure environment. In fact, the mainframe computer is now enjoying a new lease of life by supporting some of the largest Internet-based trading systems in the world.

Many of the most successful companies throughout the world still store huge amounts of business-critical data on mainframes. In an industry where everyone is talking about PCs, servers and client-server computing, it is worth remembering that 60 per cent of business data still resides on mainframes. Whilst demand for mainframe skills is dwindling, demand for integration skills (ensuring applications running on legacy systems will interact with thin-client systems (see below)) is rising fast and they are now the source of many top IT jobs.

The networked PC

The day that a length of cable was used to connect two PCs, effectively creating a network, was a monumental one in the history of the PC industry. The ability to share files and printers over a network was a huge step forward, so creating the concept of a desktop PC and a PC server. The true PC network was firmly established by Novell with its Netware operating system, and despite the growing dominance of Microsoft networking products, Novell Netware is still a major platform used for networking business systems, including the Internet.

Client-server computing

Not far behind the success of the networked PC came the client-server architecture, which some people believe is the most significant change ever to affect the IT industry. The rise in client-server computing has been driven by the availability of inexpensive but powerful PC servers gradually replacing the mainframe, migrating mainframe-based applications to run from the PC server. Networked desktop PCs could now be used as powerful 'clients', accessing networked applications whilst also being capable of running complex applications locally on the PC.

Despite the obvious advantages, client-server computing has since proved to be costly – it is inherently more complex to manage and support and has potential security issues as the computing logic is dispersed throughout the organisation, rather than being centralised in one place.

Whilst the spiralling costs of maintaining client-server systems have been the bane of many company accountants, it has meant there have been huge increases in PC-based development and support roles. Skilled PC staff now form large parts of the IT hierarchy within the majority of organisations. Similarly, IT staff who work for software development companies who produce system management tools for client-server environments have also enjoyed high salaries and good career development.

Thin-client computing

With the availability of software development tools that allow Web-based systems to be implemented easily, more and more organisations are now viewing the Internet as a medium on which they can deploy their applications. User access to the Internet is the key factor in these new application systems by means of a Web browser or Internet portal.

The structure of the IT industry

The IT profession has, at its core, the software and hardware sectors, which are fundamental in the development of all computer systems used today. Figure 2.1 should give you an indication of the structure of the IT industry within the European Union (EU).

On a global scale, companies are continually seeking to gain commercial advantage by adopting new technology. As a result, there has been a phenomenal rise in other industry sectors that have a strong affinity to IT, namely media and telecommunications. The combination of these three key sectors has now produced a new sector, the technology, media and telecommunications (TMT) sector, which includes some of the most successful organisations in the UK. This is good news for anyone seeking a top job in IT, as there is a high level of interworking between them (see Figure 2.2 on page 22).

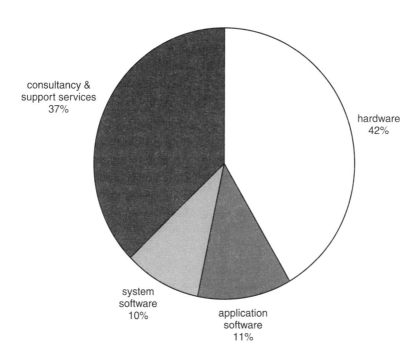

Figure 2.1 The structure of the IT industry within the European Union

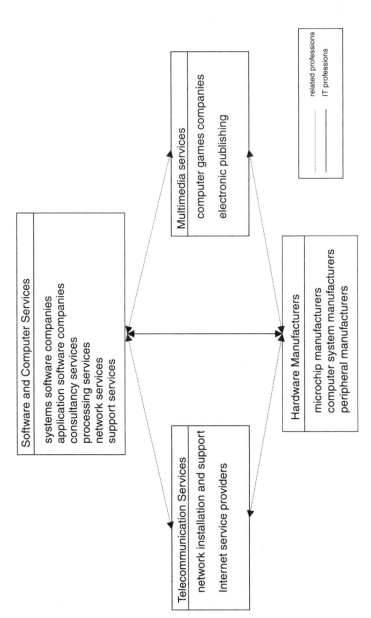

Figure 2.2 The TMT sector

3 Working in software and professional services

Of all the areas within the IT industry, the software and professional services sector is the one which employs the most people and will probably be the best place to find a top job in IT. Its size and importance in terms of employment potential means the software and services sector is an area you should consider very carefully before deciding on any specific career path. It is estimated that more than 16,000 software and services companies, employing over 300,000 staff, exist in Western Europe alone. On top of this, additional employment is emerging with the development of the Internet and multimedia applications.

Systems software

This area concerns the programs and utilities that control the computer's processes, such as input/output, file handling, security and networking. Collectively, these programs and utilities are referred to as the operating system.

Operating system software, unlike application software, is not substantially developed or upgraded on a regular basis and so the majority of work in this sector is focused around issues such as improving security, performance and fault diagnosis and repair. Historically, operating systems were written in low-level programming languages such as assembler, but many of the more popular operating systems (such as UNIX, Linux and NT) are now either completely written in, or have many sub-routines written in, languages such as C. Whilst it is always a good idea to have strong skills in the underlying language of the operating system, many of the more common system-related functions performed by systems programmers are included in specialist software tools.

These allow access into key parts of the operating system and allow important parameters and modules to be amended. Obviously, these are not the sorts of activities you would want everyone in the IT department to be allowed to perform, so security and access are extremely important issues in this area.

Whilst the majority of mainframes run IBM's MVS operating system, the systems software sector is flourishing with the increase in the UNIX, Microsoft NT and Windows 2000 operating systems, which are used on smaller, multi-user systems. Working in the systems software sector allows you to work in two main areas of IT: as a systems programmer working for an end-user or consultancy or professional services organisation; or as a systems programmer working for a systems software tool vendor. Both require a high level of technical skill and understanding relating to the underlying functions and characteristics of the operating system, and often the hardware it runs on.

Obviously, every IT site is different, each may have different hardware, operating system software and vastly different levels of system complexity, but all have a common requirement: to ensure the protection and smooth running of their IT systems – and ultimately of the business processes they support. There is a much greater awareness of the service the IT department provides to its customers; the delivery and management of IT services within an organisation is often a key performance indicator to assess the value of IT within the organisation. You can see already why many IT employers now need to see evidence of business skills as well as strong IT skills, even for a job that seems extremely technical, such as systems programming.

Service management and service delivery are crucial roles within the IT department as they provide the link between key technical staff, such as systems programmers who manage and maintain the IT systems and the business, who use the applications running on them. Unfortunately, despite all the latest technological advances in hardware and software, IT systems do occasionally fail, leaving the business struggling to continue working, for instance by having to process orders manually or revert to contingency procedures. For this reason, the technical staff working for an end-user organisation may well have to ensure the IT systems they manage adhere to a service-level agreement (SLA). SLAs are becoming commonplace now for many good reasons – for one, it gives the business an assurance that the key applications it needs to function will be available at specific times (often all day, every day of the year, or '24 × 7'). Whilst shift working is not always necessary in this sector, most IT professionals working at this level would be expected to provide some form of out-of-hours support, either by phone or by remote working for simple problems and being onsite for more serious ones.

Application software

Without application software, the most powerful computers in the world are of little use to anyone – it is software that provides the business user with the applications they need to trade and compete successfully in the marketplace. The majority of this software provides business users with the capability to retrieve, manipulate and store business information quickly and easily (business people are not necessarily computer experts). Application software can be designed to run for one user on a PC, such as a database or word-processing package, or it can be designed to run for hundreds of users on large computer systems, where the application software might run the stock control system or the company's Web site.

Despite the advances in e-commerce, super-PCs and object-oriented programming, the majority of business applications still run on mainframe computers; and most of those are written in COBOL, a so-called 'legacy' programming language that is decades old. True, COBOL applications are now gradually being replaced by applications written in languages such as Visual Basic, Visual C++ and Java, but mainframe-based applications will always exist mainly because they can store and process huge amounts of information extremely quickly, unlike most PCs. If you need convincing, you might want to take a closer look at some of those smart, flashy Web sites that promote some of the biggest UK organisations. Behind that flashy Web interface, it is highly likely that the core business processing functions are still being performed by a COBOL program, working like the clappers!

Consultancy services

As the number of applications, technologies and strategies developed by the IT industry increases, so too does the number of options available to business. For instance, what computer platforms should the business use to develop or expand its IT capability? Is the business problem big enough to warrant a very expensive mainframe or will a cluster of powerful PC servers do the same job for less? How can the business take advantage of the Internet?

There are, of course, hundreds of other issues that organisations seek to resolve with the help of an IT consultancy organisation (whether to buy an 'off-the-shelf' software package or develop their own 'bespoke' application is a common one). Similarly, many organisations need specific help and advice on integrating new software with existing systems (especially in the e-commerce area). None of these questions can be answered easily without understanding the organisation's specific business requirements – both in the short-term and in the long-term (computer systems can become obsolete *very* quickly, so some thought must be taken when deciding what to buy).

Professional services such as project management, application design and development are provided by the majority of consultancies; there are considerably fewer companies who can provide advice on specialist areas such as global e-commerce, IT security and global risk management. Only the very largest consultancy companies (such as IBM) can provide professional services covering every aspect of IT.

IT consultancy companies work closely with the customer to identify their business requirements and the best ways of achieving them. In many respects, they perform many, if not all of the IT functions found within other organisations, such as programming, analysis, technical support and project management. Consultancy companies are growing in size all the time, many have customers worldwide and utilise all the latest technologies; the opportunities they can offer graduates are some of the best in the industry.

The latest annual survey of the top IT consulting firms (see Table 3.1) shows that fee income remains high, fuelling demand for

Table 3.1 The top 10 IT consulting firms ranked by fee income during 1999

Rank	Consultancy Firm	1999 Fee Income (£million)
1	Andersen Consulting	166.2
2	PricewaterhouseCoopers	155.0
3	ICL Group	71.3
4	Sema	69.5
5	Logica	59.4
6	PA Consulting Group	53.5
7	CSC	48.1
8	Deloitte Consulting	47.7
9	IBM	41.4
10	KPMG	37.5

(Source: *Management Consultancy*)

extra consultancy staff. The leading players in the full table share well over 40 per cent of the total market and the top 10 share around two-thirds of the market. This is a clear indication that when it comes to consultancy companies, the bigger they are, the better.

The consultancy model

If you take the time to read magazines such as *Computer Weekly* and *Management Consultancy* you will soon discover that there is a plethora of consultancy firms operating within the IT industry. Whilst they all may appear to be offering similar services, they may actually operate completely differently to their competitors, both in terms of the services they offer and the markets they operate within.

Large consultancies such as IBM Global Solutions, Cap Gemini Ernst & Young (both companies merged during 2000), EDS and Logica will operate within many business sectors, such as telecommunications, defence, health, finance and industry, and their businesses will be structured to meet the specific needs of each sector. Consultancy firms who are large enough to operate in this way will normally have a pool of consultants available at any time from which they can resource specific projects (see Figure 3.1). Usually consultants in the pool will have specialist knowledge of one or more business sectors, although movement between sectors is always possible with training (and is often encouraged).

Outsourcing companies

Simply put, outsourcing is paying another company (a consultancy company in most cases) to perform the tasks normally

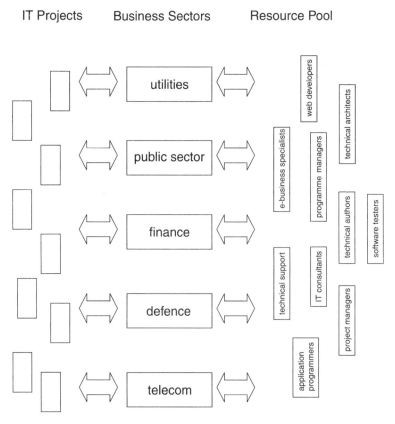

Figure 3.1   The consultancy model

undertaken by an organisation's IT department. Companies can outsource different tasks to different outsourcing providers or, as is becoming increasingly popular, they can outsource everything to them; from desktop PC management and support to the complete management of every IT function within the business.

Outsourcing is big business, and therefore one can assume there is huge potential in this area for some sparkling careers. According to the _Holway Report_, an annual guide to IT software and services by the analyst group Richard Holway Limited, spending on outsourcing was expected to increase by 14 per cent during 2000. While this is a sharp fall from 1998's figure of 25 per cent, one of the highest spending companies in 1999 topped £900 million (see Table 3.2). The growth in the outsourcing market is not surprising; on the one hand companies are entering new markets, particularly those related to e-commerce, yet on the other, the skills shortage in the industry is around 20 per cent, rising to nearly 40 per cent in the e-commerce sector.

Table 3.2 The top 10 IT outsourcers in 1999

Rank	Company	UK Outsourcing Revenue (£million)
1	EDS	950
2	IBM	700
3	CSC	426
4	Cap Gemini	368
5	Sema	311
6	ICL	280
7	Capita	245
8	Andersen Consulting	157
9	FI Group	153
10	Siemens SBS	152

(Source: _Holway Report_ 2000)

Company profile: EDS

EDS is the UK's largest outsourcing provider, with a reported revenue of $20 billion during 1999–2000. Of this figure, approximately $1.5 billion was generated in the UK, representing an increase of 14 per cent in its performance since 1998. This is an impressive figure, but pales into insignificance when you realise that IBM Global Services grew by a staggering 32 per cent during the same period.

Historically, EDS has operated mainly for large organisations within the public sector, such as the Prison Service and the Inland Revenue. In the private sector, their customers include companies such as Rolls-Royce. EDS offers a wide range of IT outsourcing options (and therefore good career entry and development options), from desktop management to full outsourcing (all IT systems and services) and project management. The majority of its business, however, comes from these larger projects – the typical EDS customer has an annual turnover in excess of $100 million (£63 million).

The outsourcing market is changing just as fast as the rest of the IT industry, and EDS expects its core business to change as a result too. It already estimates that within five years its customers will be demanding 'functionality-on-demand'-type contracts, accounting for 40 per cent of its business.

In the shorter term however, EDS's fastest growing source of revenue is business process outsourcing, where it takes responsibility for business functions rather than IT functions.

Company profile: IBM Global Services

IBM is the world's largest provider of outsourcing services, with revenues of $32 billion in 1999. It also leads the European market, but trails EDS in the UK. This situation is likely to change fairly soon as IBM is growing at a huge rate within the UK.

IBM specialises in vertical sectors, such as banking, communications, retail, industrial and pharmaceutical (*cf* the consultancy model). Typical customers include Cable & Wireless Communications, which was also the largest ever UK outsourcing deal when it was signed in 1998.

IBM does have one major advantage over most of its rivals in the outsourcing market: as well as traditional outsourcing, it can also offer software, hardware services and training. All these add up to some excellent careers, both in the UK and internationally.

IBM's outsourcing business is split into four divisions:

- Traditional outsourcing covers (application) hosting, facilities and network management. Despite the 'old hat' label, this area still forms the bulk of IBM's business.
- Systems Integration offers business intelligence and technical consulting.
- IT Services covers technical solutions.
- e-Learning, IBM's latest training division, was launched early 2000.

Software development in action

There are lots of business problems that cannot be solved by the use of computer software, which is why a career within software development can be such an interesting and rewarding one. When writing business software, it is crucial that you first understand the needs and requirements of the business and are able to identify the technical solution necessary to solve its problems. This is just the start of a lengthy process, which begins with a business requirement and ends with a delivered computer solution. It is called the system development lifecycle (SDLC).

Object-oriented development

Object-oriented development is now a major software development methodology as it promotes the development of reusable, portable and interoperable code. Object-oriented software design methods view a software system as a set of interacting objects rather than set of functions (which is the basis of traditional software development).

31

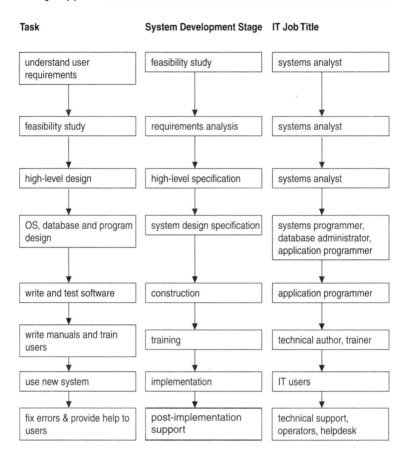

Task	System Development Stage	IT Job Title
understand user requirements	feasibility study	systems analyst
feasibility study	requirements analysis	systems analyst
high-level design	high-level specification	systems analyst
OS, database and program design	system design specification	systems programmer, database administrator, application programmer
write and test software	construction	application programmer
write manuals and train users	training	technical author, trainer
use new system	implementation	IT users
fix errors & provide help to users	post-implementation support	technical support, operators, helpdesk

Figure 3.2 The systems development lifecycle

Object-oriented development is encapsulated in Microsoft's Component Object Model (COM) and Distributed COM (DCOM), which are popular amongst many IT organisations. Whether you like it or not, Microsoft, for the moment at least, has the power to dictate the way forward in IT software development and is constantly reviewing its development strategies. ActiveX is one such strategy, and it is a generic term applied to Microsoft's technologies for creating and using software components. Many of the individual terms and technologies used within this area used to be largely interchangeable, but with the evolution of ActiveX Controls and ActiveX Data Objects the definitions have become more precise. ActiveX forms a part of Microsoft's COM, which is a software architecture that allows applications to be built from binary software components. The concept behind the strategy is simple: if you can build your application by reusing or modifying existing pieces of software (software components) you can reduce the effort and cost involved in large-scale application development. Additionally, component technology also helps reduce the problems caused by integrating existing code into new applications.

Be aware, though, that whilst Microsoft is the leading player in component-based development, COM and ActiveX are not the only approach. Many organisations that decide not to develop Microsoft-based systems can still adopt component-based techniques using technologies such as CORBA and Enterprise Java Beans, which can seamlessly integrate with ActiveX as well as each other. CORBA is an independent, cross-platform standard that provides a single infrastructure for distributed application integration, which is managed by the Object Management Group.

To enter the world of component-based development you will need at least a basic grasp of C++ and/or Visual C++ and some knowledge of component building and deployment. If you are seeking a top job in application development, this might be a good area to choose, as Microsoft developers with COM/ActiveX skills are highly sought after. As a rough guide, people with these skills are currently being headhunted by agencies, attracting salaries of about £35,000. Even if you have only one year's CORBA or COM experience with solid C++ skills, you could easily attract a salary of £30,000+. The ORB Agency specialises in recruitment for object-oriented development. It can be contacted on (020) 8847 2929 or at its Web site: www.orbagency.com.

Key recruiters

—— Company profile: Oracle Corporation ——

The Oracle Corporation is the world's largest supplier of database software and information management software, with annual revenues of over $4.2 billion. Oracle software, whilst often associated with UNIX systems, runs on almost every computer, from the smallest laptop to the massively powerful super-computers.

In addition to providing database and Internet development software, Oracle also provides consultancy services. Oracle Consulting has over 5,000 consultants working in Europe, the Middle East and Africa, recruited from all walks of industry. Combined with their industry-specific experience and a thorough knowledge of Oracle products, they are able to advise and assist customers on the implementation of Oracle technology.

Oracle UK is a wholly-owned subsidiary of the Oracle Corporation and employs over 4,500 people in 10 regional locations. Oracle UK has a European Porting Centre at Blackrock, Ireland, from where it transfers (ports) its software onto different computer operating systems.

Career opportunities
Oracle UK recruits graduates from many different disciplines as well as computer science, all having proven academic success in a relevant area. Normally only 10 per cent of applicants are invited for an interview, during which candidates will be expected to sit psychometric tests.

Contact information
The best place to obtain information on Oracle and current career opportunities is from its Web site: www.oracle.com/uk.

Alternatively, contact:

Human Resources Department
Oracle UK Corporation Limited
Oracle Parkway
Thames Valley Park
Reading
Berkshire RG6 1RA
Tel: (0118) 924 0000

Company profile: PA Consulting

PA Consulting provides consultancy services to blue-chip clients throughout the UK and the rest of the world. The company itself, as you might expect, is relatively large, but it has an even greater ambition – to double in size by 2002. This is great news for anyone seeking top consultancy positions with one of the world's leading consultancy firms.

Career opportunities

As with many of the top consultancy firms, PA Consulting works with global clients operating in all parts of industry, commerce and the public sector. To successfully complete strategic and operational projects in these areas, it must recruit graduates of the highest calibre, ie those who expect to gain a minimum 2:1 honours degree. For experienced professionals, PA Consulting will expect a high level of commercial acumen gained from blue-chip organisations or other consultancy firms.

Whilst PA Consulting does require a wide range of skilled professionals for the many positions available within the company, it would be particularly interested in those graduates studying for, or having recently obtained, degrees in Computer Science, Applied Technology or Business Strategy and Marketing. Career progression within PA Consulting is based on merit, with promotion from Consultant/Principal Consultant/Managing Consultant/Partner.

PA Consulting has offices in Cambridge, Glasgow, Birmingham, London and Manchester, but you are expected to be fully mobile within the UK and internationally. A flexible approach to working hours is also expected.

Contact information

The best place to obtain information on PA Consulting is from its corporate Web site: www.pa-consulting.co.uk.

Top jobs within software and professional services

There are very good opportunities for people wanting to work in the software and professional services sector; programmers continue to remain in demand at all levels, from junior programmers working for local government to software development consultants working for the large multinational companies.

If you want to walk straight into a consultancy role with one of the major professional IT consultancy companies such as Cap Gemini Ernst & Young, EDS, Logica, IBM and ICL, you will without doubt need a good degree. If the employer also has a graduate training programme, you will not necessarily need a degree in a computing subject – they will train you for whatever role you are best suited to.

Application development

The typical structure of roles within software development (and consultancy roles within this area) is shown in Figure 3.3.

The project manager

Most common IT development work is team-based and it is the role of the project manager to ensure the development team complete their tasks to the satisfaction of the customer within the specified time and budget. An IT project could be an internal piece of work within an organisation or it could be external to the company, working for another organisation or IT software house.

Key tasks and skills

A typical project manager does not need technical skills, although having a good understanding of IT concepts and issues is a benefit. Project managers, however, must have good communication skills as they deal with people all the time – either their own IT project team or the customer. A good project manager will listen to, understand and motivate the project team and liaise effectively with customers to ensure they are happy. A project manager is an

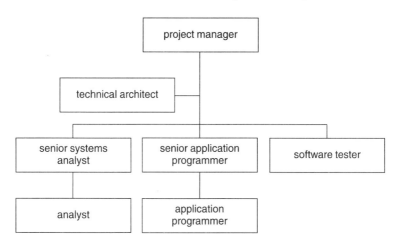

Figure 3.3 The application development team structure

unusual breed of person, hard and tough when required, yet flexible and accommodating when the need arises. Diplomacy and tact are as important in this job as hard-edged business acumen. Table 3.3 summarises the key tasks and skills for a project manager.

Throughout the duration of the project, the project manager will coordinate and control the combined efforts of the project team. As a typical project team consists of systems analysts, programmers, testers, trainers and implementers, it is important that the project manager must have a good awareness of the software development lifecycle.

Projects by their very nature consist of a number of well-defined tasks, which must be identified and tracked by the project manager. Where issues arise during the project (regardless of whether it is a technical issue or a 'people' issue), the project manager must try to resolve it as soon as possible as it might affect one of the key project measures: timescale, cost and budget.

Typically, a small project might involve three or four IT development staff working together for two or three months, maybe implementing a small software package or providing a small amount of software development. A large project might require over 200 IT staff over a period of three years.

Table 3.3 Key tasks and skills for a project manager

Key Tasks	Essential Skills	Desirable Skills
PLANNING • identifying and presenting the business case for the project; • writing the project plan; • setting key milestones to track the project; • identifying roles and responsibilities for the project; • identifying key stakeholders in the project (customers).	• experience of project management techniques; • budgeting; • negotiation.	• experience of project management software tools (eg *Microsoft Project*).
COMMUNICATION • providing the customer with regular progress reviews; • discussing key stages of the project with senior management; • ensuring all members of the project are kept informed throughout the duration of the project.	• delivering presentations; • report writing; • effective listening.	• non-verbal communication; • building a rapport with the customer.
MANAGING • managing and motivating the team; • managing the customer; • managing timescales and budget.	• leadership; • ability to delegate; • good business sense.	• negotiation; • persuasion; • team building.

Being a project manager often means juggling resources for the project (such as ensuring you have enough suitable people to work on the project) against costs (which are usually dictated by the customer) and time. If that isn't enough, a project manager will often become embroiled in the politics of the situation if working for an external customer, a situation that has only one ending – conflict!

IT project management is not an easy job – you only have to read popular IT publications such as _Computing_ and _Computer Weekly_ to get an idea of how many IT project failures there are. When things are going well technically and the customer is happy, the project manager will be the first person to offer the team a morale-boosting team drink at the local pub, but when technical problems begin to creep into the project, the project manager will need nerves of steel. When timescales slip and costs rise, the once pleasant customer will mutate into a deranged psychopath. At best, the project manager will be verbally assaulted every day until things start to improve. At worst, the project manager will find him- or herself ceremoniously dumped off the project (and possibly into a home for the bewildered).

The working environment
It is not uncommon for project managers to work beyond their contracted hours, especially when the project is reaching implementation stage or whenever the project runs into difficulty (which unfortunately seems to be quite often in the IT profession). The project manager very often cannot dictate his or her own schedule; hours worked will depend on the customer and the nature of the project to a large extent. If the project is external, the project manager will need to travel to and from the customer site, usually to attend project review meetings.

Salary
Graduate project managers: £22,000–£25,000.
Experienced project managers: £25,000–£50,000.
Experienced freelance project managers: anything from £2000/week upwards.

Entry, training and career development
Traditionally, many project managers have come from either an IT development or analysis background or have commercial and

business project management experience. Such is the demand however for project managers, many of the larger IT consultancy companies now train IT graduates for project management roles working on client sites. Whilst project managers do not necessarily need a degree qualification in an IT-related subject, the better ones have been on accredited Project Management training courses, such as those run by the Information Systems Examination Board (ISEB) or the Cranfield School of Management. Postgraduate qualifications, such as an MSc, can be useful for the aspiring project manager as many courses cover the management of IT projects in the syllabus. Further details on ISEB and other training institutions can be found in Chapter 12.

Anne *is a Project Manager working for a consultancy company.*

Project management is a very demanding but rewarding role. Sure, when things on the project go wrong (such as timescales that need to be extended), I usually get the blame (even when it's not my fault), but at the same time, when my project is implemented on time, within budget and the users actually like the system, I get a huge buzz from it. I'll be honest, I've heard of ego-less programming from my IT degree course, but I've never yet heard of ego-less project management!

Whilst I did gain a degree in computer science from Manchester University, I've never really considered myself to be a technical 'geek'. I've always been interested in the interaction between technology and people – which is why I think I've been quite successful as a project manager. When I left university, I joined a large, international consultancy organisation, who immediately sent me to their management training centre – not more lectures I thought! Quite the opposite actually – I learnt some really useful business and financial skills from some fairly senior consultants who had worked with some of the largest organisations in the UK.

The key to project management is communication; ensuring everyone knows what's going on and why. Too many projects fail because IT project teams don't appreciate the requirements and issues of the business (and vice versa). As I said

---

earlier, I'm not a technical person, but I know enough about IT to be able to communicate with my IT team whilst also being able to relate to the business users at the same time. I'm quite excited at the moment as I'm starting to work on a number of e-commerce projects. It's a new challenge, and I just hope I come out of it with a few more strings to my bow!

The IT consultant

Anyone enjoying the rather grand title of consultant can be working in just about any organisation within the IT industry, performing just about any role. In the more popular interpretation of the term, however, a consultant is someone who works for one of the many management consultancies, software houses or large IT consultancy companies. Management consultancy companies traditionally tended to specialise in business and accounting consultancy, but many are now big providers of IT consultancy. Many of you might recognise KPMG and PriceWaterhouseCoopers and Ernst & Young (now merged with Cap Gemini) as accountancy companies – they are, but they are also some of the largest IT consultancy companies in the country.

Key tasks and skills

IT consultants give independent and objective advice on how best to use IT to meet specific business objectives. These could include harnessing new technology to develop leading-edge products or to make more cost-savings by improving existing business systems. A consultant's main tasks would therefore involve a high level of interaction with key business staff and managers. Depending on the nature of the project, a consultant could also be used to provide expert technical knowledge relating to IT hardware or software. As you can see from Table 3.4, a consultant must be able to draw on skills and experience from a wide range of commercial and technical areas. These skills do not come easily. University courses have often been criticised by the top consultancy firms for not providing graduates with social and communication skills that can be readily used in a business environment. Fortunately, most universities have now got the message and

Table 3.4 Key tasks and skills for an IT consultant

Key Tasks	Essential Skills	Desirable Skills
PLANNING • identifying customer requirements; • identifying best practice; • identifying project objectives.	• time management; • people management; • solid technical or managerial skills in a specific area; • project experience.	• specific knowledge of industry sectors that you might want to work in, such as defence, industry, telecommunications and finance; • some appreciation of IT finance.
COMMUNICATION • building relationships with business colleagues and external suppliers; • making objective judgement; • discussing issues with peers and superiors within own company and within client's company.	• delivering presentations; • report writing; • effective listening; • explaining technical issues clearly.	• non-verbal communication; • building a rapport with the customer.
MANAGING • managing and motivating the team; • managing the customer; • managing timescales and budget.	• leadership; • ability to delegate; • good business sense.	• negotiation; • persuasion; • team building.

there is now an equal emphasis placed on social skills as well as academic qualification within degree programmes. In the early years of being a consultant, it is the people who can master these skills and utilise them effectively that will enjoy the greatest success.

The working environment

A typical consultant works closely with the customer on their site, usually as part of a project team supplied by the consultancy company. Flexibility in working hours and location is fairly important as it is quite possible a consultant could be assigned to a project anywhere within the UK, and in the case of the large, international companies, anywhere in the world. Living away from home on a regular basis is quite common for the average consultant. Having said that, most, if not all consultancies have sites scattered throughout the UK, and there is a good chance that you will have a local office as your base (important for tax reasons and expenses!). Again, this is no guarantee that you will spend all your time in the office. Many of the consultancy firm's clients will expect any development or consultancy work to be performed on their premises.

If frequent UK and international travel appeals to you, a consultancy role with the larger companies who have clients worldwide would be a good career move. If you prefer to work with just UK-based companies, many of whom operate within well-defined geographic boundaries, a role within some of the smaller consultancy companies would be better, reducing the amount of travelling and nights spent away from home. Whilst shift-working is not performed in this role, as project deadlines approach you will be expected to 'do whatever is necessary' to ensure the project timescales are met.

Salary

Graduate consultants tend to earn between £18,000 and £22,000. Experienced consultants can expect to earn anything from £35,000 to £100,000.

Freelance management and IT consultants working within the finance and banking sector can expect to earn well over £2000 a week.

Entry, training and career development

Most consultants are recruited and trained as part of graduate recruitment and induction programmes. In the larger consultancy companies an IT degree is not essential; overall business awareness and the ability to combine IT technologies to satisfy business problems are more important.

For a long time, there has been very little formal training in consultancy skills; however, the British Computer Society (BCS) is now proposing a Certificate in Consultancy Skills course. The course will not only cover the basics in consultancy, but also techniques such as personal and presentation skills, plus issues ranging from managing assignments to running a consultancy practice. Further details of the course can be found in Chapter 12.

Career progression is fairly standard throughout the consultancy profession. Everyone is a consultant as far as the customer is concerned, but internally, promotion through the consultancy grades is normally based on length of service and performance. After gaining experience, many consultants begin to specialise in either technical consultancy, management consultancy or project

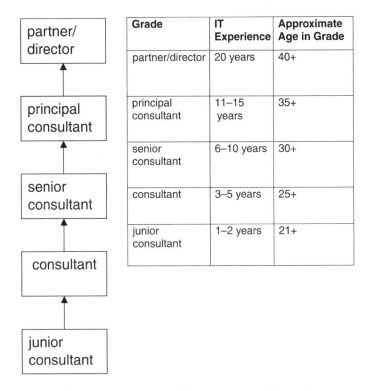

Grade	IT Experience	Approximate Age in Grade
partner/director	20 years	40+
principal consultant	11–15 years	35+
senior consultant	6–10 years	30+
consultant	3–5 years	25+
junior consultant	1–2 years	21+

Figure 3.4 Career progression within the average IT consultancy

management, eventually becoming acknowledged experts in their particular field. Figure 3.4 provides a typical career progression path for a consultant.

> **Gary _is an IT consultant working for a major European consultancy company._**
>
> I graduated from Cambridge after studying History, with no consuming desire to work within the IT profession. However, I was very impressed by the presentations given by a number of top consultancy companies, such as IBM, KPMG and PA Consulting in my final year, so I took the plunge and became a consultant.
>
> I was initially concerned that unless an organisation happened to be in need of an historian (unlikely), I would have very little to do. I need not have worried, the company was thoroughly professional and saw me as an asset from day one. During the first few tentative months, I was sent to the graduate 'academy' where I learnt some very useful business and IT skills. Of course, this did not make me a consultant overnight, which is why I was assigned a mentor who guided me through my first few projects, explaining procedures and best practice as the project developed. For me, the main benefit of being a consultant is that my skills and experiences are always growing as the result of the varied work I perform. So far I've travelled extensively throughout the UK on business and have recently worked on a small project in the US. Despite what you might think, it's not a holiday – my daily rate to the client is high and they expect their money's worth!

Further information

Whatever your level of experience, the Institute of Management Consultancy (IMC) can offer professional help and advice. Through the IMC, you can become a Certified Management Consultant, the only competency-based qualification for practising consultants. If you wanted to become a freelance management consultant (assuming you had a few years' experience of consultancy), the CMC qualification would give you an internationally recognised qualification to practise on your own. For a detailed information pack, contact the IMC at:

5th Floor
32–33 Hatton Garden
London
EC1N 8DL
Tel: (020) 7242 2140

The technical architect

In the often routine and faceless world of the IT professional, technical architects have many reasons to be fairly satisfied with their lot. Their job title, for one, is often the envy of programmers and analysts alike and their job description is wide and varied, often becoming involved with all the latest technologies and methods.

Computing and IT today is a complex affair, with projects often taking years to complete at a cost of millions. Its similarity with the construction industry has not gone completely unnoticed and in some ways the IT profession is gradually adopting many of the practices found within it. The idea of an IT 'architect', pouring over blueprints for a new system, deciding which techniques and materials to use and then sculpting and crafting the construction to ensure it complies with industry rules and best practices does conjure up some magnificent thoughts.

Key tasks and skills

Technical architects come in many shapes and sizes. Some are highly technical, expert in fact, in specific technologies or integrated solutions. Others operate at a more strategic level, becoming a technical design authority throughout the lifecycle of the project, ensuring the planning, development, testing and implementation stages are performed without any technical problems. Where problems do arise, for instance when there is a high level of integration work required to implement a software solution, the technical architect will have to measure the impact and risk of the problem, both in technical terms and in business terms before determining the best course of action. It is not unknown for a technical architect to recommend that a project be cancelled if the technical issues cannot be resolved (a quick glance at the daily newspapers will give you an idea of how many immensely complex software projects run into difficulties, such as the Passport Agency fiasco). Table 3.5 summarises the key tasks and skills for an IT architect.

The working environment

A technical architect can be involved very early on in an IT project, working closely with the project manager and members of the project team until the system is tested and implemented. Whilst many roles within the project team start and finish at prescribed stages throughout the project (such as testing), the technical architect will often provide the continuity between the stages of the project lifecycle. Most, if not all, of the work performed by a technical architect is performed during 'standard' working hours – there is no shift working and no out-of-hours support work involved. During the testing and imple-mentation phases of the project, the technical architect will perform a key role – if things have gone wrong then many long hours may be necessary to ensure problems are identified and resolved quickly.

Entry, training and career development

Most technical architects come from a technical background, such as programming, hardware or software support, or networking. However, analysis skills are often important in this role, so it is also likely that experienced business analysts could move into this role. Technical architects can expect a good amount of training, aimed at managers and senior technicians, rather than hands-on training, as they must be aware of any issues relating to using or integrating IT technologies. These skills are usually very marketable and career development is often more rapid in this role than in standard development roles.

Salary

Technical architects can expect to start on around £25,000. Experienced architects, especially those working on Internet projects, can expect to earn between £50,000 and £100,000.

Table 3.5 Key tasks and skills for an IT architect

Key Tasks	Essential Skills	Desirable Skills
ANALYSIS • modelling business functions; • modelling data flows and data stores within the business; • capturing business requirements (strategic and operational); • helping the project manager reinforce the business case for the project.	• methodical, structured approach to work; • knowledge of IT strategy; • knowledge of IT design and implementation techniques.	• experience in using data and business modelling packages (such as Oracle Designer 2000 or Corporate Modeller); • experience of systems analysis methodologies (such as Yourdon, Gane and Sarson, Information Engineering).
COMMUNICATION • ongoing relationship with users; • delivering presentations to business users and managers; • chairing review meetings with users and managers.	• effective communication: expressing your thoughts clearly, either written or verbally; • customer-facing (business jargon for being well-presented and professional when dealing with customers).	• able to articulate technical ideas and concepts to non-IT people. • building a rapport with the customer; • commercial awareness; • financial awareness.
PROBLEM SOLVING • identifying issues and risks which may influence the overall design of the system; • developing alternative solutions to meet the problem; • escalating serious design or implementation problems to the project manager and business sponsor.	• being able to work with users to resolve problems – you cannot put your head in the sand; • the ability to think calmly and make rational decisions in a high-pressure, high-profile environment.	• negotiation skills; • assertiveness; • empowerment.

Dave _is a technical architect._

When I graduated, I'd never even heard of the role I'm now performing. Like most of my colleagues, I expected to move into an analysis or programming job when I left university. I think my degree in computer science has helped me considerably in this role, as it has a large scope, covering all aspects of the systems development lifecycle as well as all the technical issues relating to hardware, software and networking.

I'm no expert, and new products and strategies are coming out all the time, which is why I attend all the major IT conferences and seminars given by the leading IT vendors. As a technical architect I am expected to know what's going on in the IT world; quite a bit of pressure as my opinion is often sought after by the IT director and senior management. That sort of pressure though, I like – it keeps my skills and knowledge up to date and I feel more confident with every project I complete.

The testing consultant

Testing is probably the most important stage within the software development lifecycle, but is often the one that is compromised first when timescales or budgets are in jeopardy. One of the reasons testing is sometimes only covered lightly during an IT project is because there are few people who can perform the role well. Good testers are hard to come by – it is a highly skilled role (see Table 3.6). Many organisations wrongly assume that a good application programmer will make a good application tester. Unfortunately, they only discover the real truth the hard way when things go wrong.

Thanks to the visibility of testing during many millennium 'bug' projects, testing is now seen as an important part of an IT project. What makes testing the specialised role it is, is partly due to the fact that it is quite difficult to train a software tester – you cannot gain a degree in testing, nor are there many (good) training courses which cover the subject in sufficient detail.

Table 3.6 Key tasks and skills for a testing consultant

Key Tasks	Essential Skills	Desirable Skills
PLANNING • designing test plans; • defining test plans; • planning overall test strategies.	• experience of formal testing (not necessarily within IT); • a logical, precise mind; • scheduling inter-related testing activities; • identifying dependencies between tasks.	• experience of specific automated test tools such as *Win-runner, X-runner* and *Rationale Robot.*
COMMUNICATION • providing application or system designers with test results and conclusions; • liaising with business users to ensure testing meets business requirements and test values and volumes are representative.	• delivering presentations; • report writing; • effective listening.	• non-verbal communication; • building a rapport with the customer.
MANAGING • ensuring testing is performed in accordance with the project plan; • ensuring the testing function involves the right people (including customers and senior business managers if necessary).	• time management; • prioritising work; • identifying issues and risks which may jeopardise the project plan.	• managing and motivating staff (especially in senior positions); • experience of providing testing expertise on multiple projects.

The working environment

Testing consultants will usually work in development teams alongside the application developers to ensure all parts of the program are covered and thoroughly tested. With the use of automated testing tools, much of the mundane work has been eliminated in testing, but it still requires a lot of skill to plan and execute the tests in the first place. Most testing is normally done within the standard working day, although there might be occasions where testing has to be performed outside these times to ensure the business is not affected by the tests.

Salary

Salaries for testing consultants can vary enormously, depending on the type and location of the work. For a testing role within the finance sector (London) an experienced testing consultant can easily earn £30,000–£40,000 a year. Graduate testing consultants working for some of the larger software testing companies can expect to earn around £18,000–£23,000 a year.

Entry, training and development

Some of the best IT testers often come from non-IT backgrounds. Science graduates seem to do particularly well in this area although there is no reason why graduates from art-based subjects could not become successful testing consultants. For similar reasons, mature graduates with postgraduate qualifications (again, not necessarily in an IT subject) often make excellent test consultants. A sensible and methodical approach to work is key to success in this role. If you are the type of person who is only motivated by developing leading edge solutions in all the latest programming languages, this is probably not the role for you.

I'll be honest, being a testing consultant will not turn heads at parties (as might an Enterprise Java Beans programmer at some of the sadder IT parties); in fact, at times it is probably fairly boring. But, in terms of importance, your rational, logical mind could literally save the organisation millions of pounds by highlighting errors early on in the system's development lifecycle.

Career progression is good – with more and more new technologies in use (such as e-commerce), the need for experienced testers will become even greater. Freelance testing is where the money is, and you only have to look in the popular IT magazines to get an idea of its worth. One freelance testing consultant I knew was quite pleased with her career to date – she earned more than the IT manager she worked for and drove a Porsche.

Judith *is a software testing consultant.*

I'll be honest, my background is not in IT. I studied Geology at Durham University where I had aspirations of becoming a surveyor working in the oil industry! By the time I graduated though, I realised that the future of the oil industry was far from certain, so I decided to move into the IT industry. As my logic and mathematics skills were good (which I thought would be useful for programming), I decided to get some general IT skills by completing an MSc conversion course in IT. The course was very much oriented towards IT management, such as planning enterprise systems and network design, which gave me a really good set of skills pitched at the right level for me.

My first IT job was as an analyst with a UK bank. I enjoyed it immensely as it consolidated many of the academic skills I had, but after a while I realised I needed a new challenge. I decided to join an IT consultancy, not a large one, but a specialist in providing banking software, as a software tester. I'm sure my banking experience helped, but the role was perfect for me. As you can imagine, testing complex banking and financial systems is not easy, but I enjoyed the challenge and the responsibility. In some ways, I found I learnt more about the IT systems by testing them than I would if I was just writing them. It does take a great amount of effort to devise a test that will have sufficient coverage to test every possible execution path within the program. To be honest, I was expecting this role to be fairly plain and uneventful, but I'm finding I'm increasing my skills in my other areas as well. Sure, I'm no programming expert, but I'm becoming aware of many of the language-specific issues that need to be tested in many of the popular programming languages such as Java and C++.

The systems analyst

The role of the systems analyst is probably one of the most challenging within the IT industry. Over the years, the rather simple role of the systems analyst has evolved to meet the growing demands and complexities of the business world, especially as a result of the new 'global economy' formed from the explosion of the Internet. A systems analyst is often a generic title for a role encompassing many analysis techniques and technologies. With the emphasis now very much on information management, the role of analyst has now evolved in a number of more specialised roles such as: information engineer, knowledge engineer, business analyst and business process consultant. It is the systems analyst who must initially convert a business requirement (such as 'we need a better order-processing system') into a series of IT requirements that application programmers and database designers will understand. Analysts often work with other IT professionals and business users as members of a project until the IT solution has been built and implemented – the systems development project.

Historically, once the analyst had produced the IT requirements, their role had, to a large extent, finished. Nowadays, many analysts also write the application code after capturing the business requirements, in essence, performing an analyst/programmer role. Analyst programmers are becoming more and more popular as many IT companies now require staff with a mixture of programming and analytical skills.

Once an IT project has started, usually with the publication of a proposal document, the systems analyst must begin to understand the customer's current system (regardless of whether it is implemented on a computer or not). Only by identifying the business processes and functions in the existing system can the analyst be confident that the new system will be developed correctly. Where a company seeks to gain competitive advantage by changing many of their business processes and functions (ie how they operate as a business) this process is called business process re-engineering (BPR). For the systems analyst working on large analysis projects such as BPR projects, it is important to remain focused on the business needs and issues and not the technical issues. Good business projects often fail because the business has been led by the technology. A successful project will be one that meets all the requirements identified by the business.

It is important that the systems analyst focuses closely on the users' requirements throughout the project and what they are expecting to be delivered at the end of it – any misunderstandings by the user or the analyst could seriously impact the success of the project. To help prevent this happening, the analyst will refer to a document produced at the start of the project, the *Terms of Reference*, which identifies the objectives and scope of the project, and clarifies exactly what is expected by the customer.

Key tasks and skills

The role of a systems analyst is often a complex one, combining many different technical and managerial skills. Much of their work involves gathering and collating information from the business in order to produce technical requirements. The systems analyst has a huge responsibility in ensuring the user requirements have been captured accurately. More importantly, it is essential for the requirements to be *understood*. There must only be one way of interpreting requirements; any ambiguity will cause problems later in the development phases. Table 3.7 summarises the key tasks and skills for a systems analyst.

After looking at this demanding list of skills, you can understand why many systems analysts have degrees or have a fair amount of business experience. Systems analysis is not an easy role in IT for the inexperienced starter – even for an IT graduate.

The working environment

Systems analysts provide an important set of skills that are required by the IT department as a whole. In an end-user organisation, such as the Post Office, analysts may exist in a team of their own, a technical 'pool' of staff, who can be utilised by other parts of the organisation when required. For larger tasks, however, or for many of the analyst roles within IT consultancy companies and software houses, the systems analyst will normally be assigned to a specific project. In the systems development lifecycle (see Figure 3.2), the analyst will work closely with the users of the new IT system throughout the early and middle stages of the project. As the project enters the build and test phases, the role of the analyst will reduce considerably. From this point the

Table 3.7   Key tasks and skills for a systems analyst

Key Tasks	Essential Skills	Desirable Skills
ANALYSIS • modelling business processes; • modelling business functions; • modelling data flows and data stores within the business; • capturing business requirements (strategic and operational); • helping the project manager reinforce the business case for the project.	• methodical, structured approach to work; • ability to elicit information from business users and managers using techniques such as: questionnaire design, structured interviewing, facilitated workshops.	• experience in using data and business modelling packages (such as Oracle Designer, Corporate Modeller or CASE tools); • experience of systems analysis methodologies (such as Yourdon, Checkland, Gane and Sarson, Information Engineering).
COMMUNICATION • ongoing relationship with users; • delivering presentations to business users and managers; • chairing review meetings with users and managers.	• effective communication – expressing your thoughts clearly, either written or verbally; • customer-facing (business jargon for being well-presented and professional when dealing with customers).	• able to articulate technical ideas and concepts to non-IT people; • building a rapport with the customer; • commercial awareness; • financial awareness.
PROBLEM SOLVING • identifying issues and risks which may influence the overall design of the system; • developing alternative solutions to meet the problem.	• being able to work with users to resolve problems – you cannot put your head in the sand.	• brainstorming techniques; • thinking 'out-of-the-box'.

analyst will probably be assigned onto another project, although it is not uncommon for an analyst to be working on a number of projects at the same time.

Entry, training and career development
Entry into systems analysis is usually more direct than the many entry paths that are available to programmers. Unless you have come from an analysis background (not necessarily in IT), you will need to have a degree. Whilst a degree in French or Biology (for example) will not provide you with analysis skills, it will, however, enable you to join a graduate entry and training programme where you will be taught structured systems analysis skills. Historically, systems analysis was considered the ideal stepping stone for a future career in IT management or project management (in the sense that programmers would find it difficult to achieve 'management' positions). This is no longer the case, but experienced systems analysts (or business analysts) are often picked up by the large IT consultancy firms, especially for strategic projects.

Salary
A graduate systems analyst can expect to earn anything between £15,000 and £20,000 a year. With experience, systems analysts can easily attract salaries in the region of £30,000–£50,000 a year.

Nimal *is a systems analyst.*

In 1987, I graduated from Sheffield Hallam University with a degree in Business Studies, with the intention of being in management by the time I was 30. I'm pleased to say that didn't happen as I'm now thoroughly enjoying my current career as a business systems analyst with a major manufacturing company, based in London. I joined the company's graduate recruitment scheme as a graduate trainee, and became a Trainee Analyst by the time the programme had completed. For the next two years I assisted in several small analysis projects, working in a small team. Although I found it interesting, I also found it difficult at first, especially when it

---

came to modelling business systems with diagrams such as entity-relationship-diagrams and dataflow diagrams. I think my business degree did help me in the early stages, as understanding the business and the user requirements is vital for this sort of work.

Gaining promotion to an Analyst, for the next four years I performed the role of lead analyst in a support environment. During that time I was responsible for documenting user requirements and producing and updating system specifications, which I passed to the programming team to code. I am now a Systems Analyst, which means I am responsible for the whole process of requirements analysis, producing functional and system specifications and terms of reference within my section. I now have to justify my decisions to the IT manager, so I have just been sent on a cost-benefit analysis course to help me. It's a demanding job, a mistake so early on in a project could put the 'cat amongst the pigeons'! In my current position, I get the chance to meet lots of people and perform my objectives with very little supervision, which is what I like. In many ways, I am responsible for many of my actions, but having been in an analysis role since joining the company, I've got a good idea how things are done!

The application programmer

Application development is the largest occupational area within IT for very good reasons – it is through application software that IT delivers most benefit to the business. Application programmers historically wrote programs in languages such as COBOL, on mainframe computers, but today, a lot of applications are written using PC-based software packages such as C++ and Java.

Key tasks and skills

Whilst programming is a skill that can be taught through education and training, successful programmers are those who can also make use of their interpersonal and managerial skills. Table 3.8 summarises the key tasks and skills for an application programmer.

Table 3.8 Key tasks and skills for an application programmer

Key Tasks	Essential Skills	Desirable Skills
PLANNING • designing a well-structured program; • defining data structures to be used by the program; • defining external interfaces to be used by the program (eg. the Internet or electronic mail).	• logical thought (try completing the popular 'logic puzzle' magazines!); • ability to produce solutions which match customer requirements (you might think it is a great piece of code – but does it do the job?); • experience of structured programming techniques (such as Michael Jackson structured programming).	• an awareness of different programming technologies (such as component-based development and object-oriented programming); • an understanding of the other roles and activities performed within the systems development lifecycle.
COMMUNICATION • working closely with analysts to ensure the application program meets the business requirements; • working closely with the database administrator to ensure data is stored and extracted by the application program in the correct manner; • working within a team of programmers.	• ability to communicate technical ideas and concepts in an understandable manner to analysts; • ability to work in a team, sharing development and testing tasks without lowering the quality of development.	• presentation skills; • report writing skills; • meeting skills.

continued opposite

Table 3.8 *continued*

Key Tasks	Essential Skills	Desirable Skills
IMPLEMENTING • writing the application code within timescales; • building application interfaces; • planning and performing unit and system testing.	• ability to produce clear, understandable and well-structured program code (someone else may have to maintain your program later); • ability to prepare and execute appropriate testing techniques.	• customer-facing skills; • experience of automated software testing tools.
PROBLEM SOLVING • resolving application and data problems; • resolving performance problems; • running diagnostic software or writing reports to assist in fault-finding and resolution.	• ability to prioritise problems • ability to manage problems; • ability to learn from mistakes; • ability to generate alternative solutions.	• ability to think laterally; • 'brainstorming' techniques (to generate ideas).

The working environment
Most application programmers usually work in a team, managed by a senior programmer. Within the team there will probably be a number of experienced application programmers and a small number of junior programmers. Whilst they will all write program code, it is likely that the experienced programmers will design and write the main parts of the application, leaving the junior programmers to write and test the smaller and less crucial parts of the application.

Entry, training and career development
Application development (especially for Internet-based applications)

is one of the main recruitment areas for IT and non-IT graduates alike. Modern day application development tools are now intuitive and extremely powerful, allowing rapid development to be performed. The benefit of such tools is fairly obvious – you don't need to be a rocket scientist to use them. In fact, it is often the case that non-IT graduates and experienced people from other disciplines prove to be better programmers than IT graduates! Sometimes having previous experience of a particular programming language or development methodology is not always helpful to employers. Many IT employers actually prefer to recruit programmers who have little or no technical experience, such as those coming from an art or media background, so they can 'mould' them in their own way.

Career development for application developers is good. Programming methods are changing all the time, so there are always new skills to learn. It is important to remember that it is the application that delivers the benefits to the organisation. In a business world where the ability to rise to the challenges of operating in an increasingly demanding global market is essential, the effectiveness and quality of the application is often where competitive advantage is made.

Salary
Graduate programmers: £16,000–£20,000.
Experienced programmers: £25,000–30,000.

Pete *is an application programmer.*

Originally, the idea of entering the computer profession was not one of my career aims, which is why I decided to study for a degree in English Language. On graduating, I realised that I did not really want to become an English teacher, so, realising that IT was going to be with us for some time, I decided to study for an MSc conversion course in Information Technology. The course allowed graduates in one discipline to grasp the basics of another subject within a year – it was an intensive course, but well worth the many hours I spent in the computer labs. I found this course really interesting, and I even managed to use some of my English skills when we studied artificial intelligence and natural language processing (getting computers to understand speech).

Feeling more confident with IT, I joined a small software house which produced IT applications for the utilities sectors. I was fortunate – the company had a graduate training programme and within six months of joining I had become proficient in Visual Basic. I soon realised the importance of writing 'structured' programs, as it not only makes them easier to design and write, but also much easier for other people to maintain as well. After 'graduating' from the IT training centre, I started to use my new skills in a small project team based in the computer building.

At first, I was just writing the odd line here and there – basically amending other people's programs to perform slightly better, but not long after, I was writing complex programs myself. At times, I find it hard to believe how far I've progressed in the IT world, when I could so easily have joined the teaching profession!

Lucy _is an Internet developer._

Yes, I'm guilty as charged, I joined the Internet bandwagon a couple of years ago and so far I have no regrets, in fact to be honest, I think I've got a really good future ahead of me! Despite all the hype about e-careers and e-developers, I still consider myself just another application programmer – the novelty of using Web-based technologies soon wears off.

I graduated from a computer science degree in 1998, having spent a sandwich year working on small Internet projects where I did a bit of HTML and Java programming. Not exactly leading edge, but it did give me my first taste of what developing applications for the Web was all about – and some commercial experience as well. On leaving university with a 2:1 honours degree, I joined a UK design and manufacturing company based in the Cotswolds – not exactly the leading edge City firm I was hoping for I'll admit, but I'm glad I did. The company already had an 'e-business' strategy in place when I joined and, so far, my career has developed strongly, allowing me to pick up new skills in Visual C++ and (Microsoft) SQL Server. As I already had some HTML skills, I found I was able to quickly fit into the programming team and contribute well.

It's funny, when asked what I do, I always reply 'I design and develop Web pages, allowing users to access information from the company's many databases', but I do a lot more than that. I've become the programming team leader for the e-business project we're working on, so I now also supervise the more junior members of the team as well – helping them understand the issues relating to writing applications for deployment on the Internet. I'm lucky, I know there is a lot of demand for people with my skills at the moment, which has meant that the company has invested a lot in training and career development to make sure I don't leave for a competitor.

Technical support

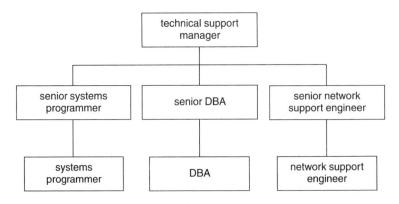

Figure 3.5 The technical support team structure

The systems programmer

Within all computer systems, there are a number of programs and utilities that are used by the computer system itself. Collectively they are called _systems software_. Writing, installing or maintaining this software is the main task performed by the systems programmer.

The systems programmer will often have to manipulate special files or execute complex commands as part of their work. Some of these commands will directly affect the operation and performance of the computer system, others will be less noticeable to the users. As with any change to an IT system, there is an element of risk inherent in the work of a systems programmer. Thousands of users may be dependent on the computer system, and it has not been unknown for mistakes at this level to cause the business to lose huge amounts of revenue as a result of the computer system being unavailable for even small periods of time.

To be fair, today's IT systems are extremely robust and security systems will ensure key parts of the system cannot be damaged accidentally. That is not to say accidents (whether man-made or not) do not happen – many organisations now have what is called a 'business continuity plan' that identifies the business and technical actions that must be performed in the event of a disaster. The disaster could be anything from a flood or fire in the computer room to an earthquake hitting the building. The systems programmer will be a key member of the 'disaster recovery' team and help build and test any contingency systems located some miles away from the main computer building.

Key tasks and skills

Table 3.9 summarises the key tasks and skills for a systems programmer.

The working environment

For those people who thrive on understanding the fundamental software components of a computer system, the systems programmer is the ultimate role. Over time, systems programmers can easily become acknowledged technical experts or gurus in specific areas, such as MVS, UNIX or NT. Being a key technical post, the systems programmer will often have many responsibilities and duties relating to the smooth running of the computer

Table 3.9 Key tasks and skills for a systems programmer

Key Tasks	Essential Skills	Desirable Skills
PLANNING • planning operating system software updates; • planning major installations of system software and utilities; • planning corrective action to resolve computer system faults.	• a methodical approach to testing; • fluency in a major piece of systems software: either an operating system (such as Microsoft NT) or a system utility.	• experience of the systems development lifecycle; • experience of project management techniques.
COMMUNICATION • working closely with programmers and other technical support staff; • explaining technical issues to non-technical staff in the department (such as help-desk staff or user representatives).	• the ability to convey often complex information accurately and timely to users and managers of the system (technical 'geeks' and 'anoraks' are no longer seen as helpful to an IT profession trying to forge greater relationships with the business).	• delivering presentations; • report writing; • effective listening.
IMPLEMENTING • installing new versions of computer software (applications and operating systems); • configuring systems software, eg data backup utilities; • tuning the computer system;	• specific (expert) knowledge of systems software tools and packages; • an advanced understanding of how computer systems function at a low level;	

continued opposite

Table 3.9   *continued*

Key Tasks	Essential Skills	Desirable Skills
• controlling access and security to the computer system.	• a humble appreciation of the power and authority this role can provide and how to be disciplined and professional enough to cope with it.	• good business sense; • teamworking.
PROBLEM SOLVING • providing second-line support when required; • resolving data problems; • resolving application performance problems; • running diagnostic software or writing reports to help identify application faults.	• solid technical skills; • good knowledge of diagnostic tools and techniques; • good communication skills.	• awareness of the key business processes and how they relate to the IT systems.

system. This will often mean the systems programmer, while not being expected to work a shift-pattern (unlike a computer operator), will often work additional hours in the evening or at weekends, when there is very little work being performed on the system.

Entry, training and career development
Traditionally, in the days of large mainframe datacentres, entry into a systems programmer role was via computer operations. It seems in those days it was considered important to have experience of refilling the paper trays in printers and loading magnetic tapes onto tape drives.

With the plethora of computer platforms and networks that are now used within the majority of IT departments, the systems programmer's role is now considered highly technical and in many cases managerial. A degree in IT is usually expected, with specific knowledge of a leading operating system, database package and/or system management tools. Unless you have knowledge of, or have undertaken specific training in, one or more specific technologies, such as UNIX, NT, MVS, Oracle or SQL Server (maybe through a vendor-specific certification programme) direct (non-IT) graduate entry into this role is difficult.

Career development is usually good in this area, as technical training is required at regular intervals to ensure systems are kept up-to-date and supportable. One word of caution, the long-haired 'hippy' mentality of systems programmers that was popular in the 70s and 80s is no longer considered professional by many leading IT and business organisations. With the IT industry constantly under fire for not getting close enough to the business, attitudes and working practices are changing. Just about any role in an IT department will now have a 'business' focus as well as a 'technical' focus; systems programming is no different. Promotion in this role will focus mainly on your technical skills, but also on your business and managerial (such as team-leading) skills.

Salary
Graduate systems programmers: £20,000–£25,000.
Experienced systems programmers: £25,000–£30,000.

Sally *is a UNIX systems programmer.*

I did a three-year BSc Chemistry course at UMIST, hoping to become an industrial chemist. I did manage to land a summer job with an ICI research station where I found to my horror that a PhD was the minimum requirement to make any reasonable progress in the chemical industry! Plan B was always going to involve a career in computing as that was a great interest of mine, although I had little commercial programming experience.

Shortly after leaving the chemical industry, I joined a medium-sized computer services company as a graduate trainee in the Operations Department. This gave me a good grounding in how a commercial computer system operates and, needless to say, I was hooked from day one. I progressed to running a shift of 12 staff running multiple machines across multiple sites and performed a wide range of tasks in many different areas, including console operations, data communications, tape handling, printing and disaster recovery.

I moved out of operations into mainframe systems programming by initially joining a small IBM consultancy company, and later by moving to the Post Office. My operations experience was essential, enabling me to program the computer systems to perform the required actions. As part of my systems programming work, I became involved in what has now become a huge area of importance – datacentre automation. Whilst it is quite complex, automation basically consists of determining the most appropriate actions (rather than those currently being carried out) and then configuring the various automation tools [system software] to perform them.

Recently I have become involved in a large project to automate and integrate all the other computer platforms used within the business, such as NT, UNIX and MVS. Within this project I found my scientific training useful for analysing operational requirements and writing various reports in a clear, objective manner.

The database administrator

Many business applications access and update large amounts of information that is stored in a database. Whilst there are many different types of databases available today, relational databases, such as Microsoft SQL Server, DB2 and Oracle, are probably the most popular. When information held in the database is added, updated or deleted by an application program, it is called a *transaction*. A good example of a transaction is the process that allows you to obtain money from an automatic teller machine (ATM) in a bank, updating the database on which your account details are held in the process. As you can imagine, over time, as more users run transactions against the database, it will gradually increase in size and if left unmanaged, will eventually cause problems. It is vitally important that the structure of the database and the complex relationships between the data are maintained regularly by the database administrator, otherwise inconsistencies could arise.

Key tasks and skills
Table 3.10 summarises the key tasks and skills for a database administrator.

The working environment
Working as a key member within technical support teams, the database administrator (DBA) has a similar work environment to the systems programmer. Whilst the DBA does not normally form part of a development team, a DBA will be expected to assist during the development stages of a project when the database requirements have been captured. A DBA will normally spend a lot of time early on in a project discussing data requirements both with the users of the application and the application programmers.

Similar to the role performed by a systems programmer, the majority of work performed by a DBA will be in the area of maintenance and support. Once an application that requires a database has gone live, the DBA will be expected to maintain the database and ensure it operates within strict performance levels. An element of on-call support or out-of-hours working might be expected for a DBA, especially on business-critical systems where the database is a crucial part of the business system.

Entry, training and career development
To work as a DBA within most large organisations, whether end-user organisations or IT consultancies, you will need a degree. Whether or not you will need a degree in an IT-related subject is difficult to say. Times are changing and many organisations now prefer to recruit non-IT graduates, even for highly technical roles such as a DBA. What is important in this role (apart from technical skills) is an understanding of how the database supports the business requirements. Acquiring database administration skills is

Table 3.10 Key tasks and skills for a database administrator

Key Tasks	Essential Skills	Desirable Skills
PLANNING • planning software updates; • planning business changes; • planning database security; • planning database archiving and recovery.	• experience of database technologies such as relational database management systems (eg Oracle, Sybase, Informix, DB2) and the less-used object-oriented database management systems (OODBMS); • knowledge of a structured query language (SQL).	• a good understanding of the operating system the database resides on, such as NT,UNIX or MVS.
COMMUNICATION • working closely with programmers and analysts to ensure the database meets requirements.	• delivering presentations; • report writing; • effective listening.	• non-verbal communication; • building a rapport with the customer.
IMPLEMENTING • building the database; • managing the customer; • managing timescales and budget.	• leadership; • ability to delegate; • good business sense.	• negotiation; • persuasion; • team building.
PROBLEM SOLVING • identifying issues and risks which may jeopardise the operation of the database; • resolving data problems; • resolving performance problems; • running diagnostic software or writing reports to help identify database or application faults.	• solid technical skills; • good knowledge of diagnostic tools and techniques; • good communication skills.	• an understanding of the software development lifecycle; • awareness of the key business processes and how they relate to the IT systems.

fairly easy these days; a five-day course will provide most of the skills you are ever likely to need on a day-to-day basis, but it is much harder to appreciate and understand the wider picture of business systems design. As an entry point, most IT graduates will have a fairly good knowledge of at least one database language and query language. Similarly, most postgraduate conversion courses in IT have at least one major database design topic in the syllabus.

Career development for a DBA can lead to more senior roles, either technically or managerially. The latter is becoming extremely popular these days, with skilled DBAs leaving end-user organisations to become database consultants with some of the leading IT consultancy providers.

Salary
Graduate database administrators: £20,000–£25,000.
Experienced database administrators: £25,000–£40,000.

Stephen *is an Oracle database administrator working for a consultancy company.*

I graduated nearly five years ago with a degree in Business Studies. At the time I wasn't struck on an IT career, although I did realise having some IT skills would be useful in business. From the milk-round at University I joined a large consultancy company as a business analyst – it seemed to fit my skills perfectly: working in IT, but using my business skills. My job involved talking to users (to capture their requirements for a new computer system) and then talking to the database designers and programmers to ensure they could actually build the required system. After a while, I realised I actually preferred the database parts of the job, rather than the 'user' side. My company were equally keen for me to move into a DBA role (apparently, DBAs are always in demand) and sent me on an Oracle DBA course. Like most courses, it can only provide you with the concepts, the rest they say, is down to experience!

I now support a number of Oracle databases on a client site (such as the databases that provide the stock control system and the ordering system). I still work with users and business analysts when new items of information need to be stored within the database and when there are problems with their application that might be database-related. If the problem is not identified as being a software 'bug' within the application, there may be a problem with the database, in which case I need to get involved. Luckily, there are a lot of tools to help me, but after a while, I tend to use my intuition! In some ways, building the database is the easy bit. Keeping it managed so it performs well (even when the amount of data stored within it increases), is the tricky bit. It's a challenge, but a very worthwhile one.

4 Working in networking and telecommunications

A brief history of telecommunications

When Alexander Graham Bell made his first telephone call over 100 years ago, he could scarcely have foreseen the profound repercussions of the communications revolution he was to unleash. The proliferation of fixed-wire telephones into most homes and offices within the West created giant telecommunications companies, most of which were state-owned. Companies such as AT&T in the US, British Telecommunications, Deutsche Telekom and France Telecom in Europe became successful in terms of increased revenues and subscriber growth. During this time the basic circuit-switching technology involved in providing a standard telephone service changed little, although electrical switches gradually replaced the cumbersome and expensive electro-mechanical switching equipment used in the early networks.

The second phase of the telecommunications revolution began about 20 years ago and resulted in the privatisation of many of the public telecommunication providers. New competition led to lower prices (particularly for long-distance calls) and the introduction of a wide range of value-added services and the arrival of the first generation of wireless services based on analogue technology.

The third and current phase began with the introduction of digital technology and the transformation of the Internet from a military/academic network into a commercial, mass-communication medium in the mid-1990s. Now the Internet itself is bringing fundamental changes to the telephone network, reducing costs and adding a host of new features and services.

The mobile Internet

There is no doubt the convergence of the Internet and mobile communications will lead to lasting changes in our society. Whether the content of our communication is voice or data, image or video, the limitations of time and location will soon no longer exist. Even now, many mobile phone vendors are predicting a future where economies and societies will become even more global and knowledge-focused.

Mobility is one of the basic requirements in an increasingly global world. Many of us spend less than half our working hours at our own workplace; meetings are no longer constrained within our own company nor our own country. It is a fact of life that domestic and international travel now play a greater part in our working lives than ever before. Closely pegged to the change in our daily activities is the growing need for mobile services and applications. Our changing lifestyles now place even greater demands on our time – we want to be able to contact our families, friends and business colleagues even when we are travelling, regardless of where we are and what time it is. It is widely predicted that there will be a steady rise in network traffic over the next 10 years, both in terms of data and voice communications (see Figure 4.1).

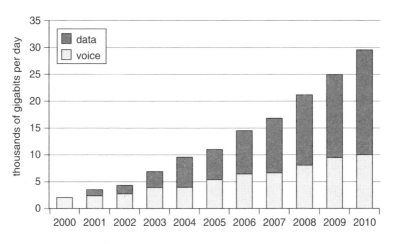

Figure 4.1 Predicted volumes of network traffic over the next 10 years

Soon, we will be using our mobile phones not only to talk, but also to send and receive digital images and videos; multimedia messaging.

Mobile computing has come a long way since the relatively cumbersome portable PCs of the 1980s. With the advancement of micro-processor technology, applications that once could only run on powerful desktop PCs can now run on a variety of hand-held computing devices (see Table 4.1). For instance, WAP technology now allows high-speed mobile data services to be accessed from WAP-enabled mobile phones. Backed by the large mobile phone manufacturers, WAP-enabled services are being marketed as 'the Internet in your pocket'. Although WAP technology does have its limitations, it does provide the ability to send emails via WAP-enabled phones and gather information such as share prices, train times or weather forecasts while on the move.

Top networking skills

A recent survey concluded that the continuing upsurge in demand for bandwidth was creating a bonanza for suppliers of networking technology (such as Cisco). Similarly, ATM (Asynchronous Transfer Mode) and frame relay technologies had seen huge rises in demand as had relatively new skills such as SDH (synchronous digital hierarchy).

WAP skills, such as WML (Wireless Markup Language), for the next few years at least will be in high demand. Questions still

Table 4.1 The history of mobile computing

1982	First 'luggable' portable PC from Compaq is available
1991	IBM enters the laptop market, joining other suppliers in an effort to catch Compaq
1992	The IBM Thinkpad is launched. A key development
1996	The first Palm Pilot is launched and rapidly becomes the most popular hand-held computer
1998	The Wireless Application Protocol (WAP) is developed, allowing Internet access for mobile phones
2000	Explosion in WAP-enabled phones capable of providing services such as share dealing and electronic mail

remain, however, as to whether WAP will be eventually replaced by another technology, such as GPRS (General Packet Radio Service). For the time being though, WAP and WML are in the limelight. Many of the popular recruitment agencies are already concerned that they are getting a lot of WAP-related vacancies that they have to satisfy with people from outside the UK.

If you have implementation experience of a WAP solution, you are in a strong position, as will having worked for some of the key mobile phone vendors such as Nokia or Ericsson. Luckily, a lot of e-banking organisations are implementing WAP solutions, so any experience of a transactional Web system will be relevant, such as security issues, Java and Web design.

One company that is pressing ahead with WAP is Graham Technology, which has created 150 new jobs to develop new customer service channels in TV, WAP and Internet environments. The company, whose clients include BT, One2One and Great Universal, are looking for applicants from various backgrounds including project managers, software engineers and graduates. The company is currently recruiting people with business consulting experience and/or pre-sales experience, as well as C++ and/or Java. New recruits will be trained to use WML. Graham Technologies can be contacted on (0141) 891 4000.

Company profile: BT plc

BT is one of the world's leading telecommunications companies, whose principal activity is the supply of local, long distance and international telecommunications services and equipment in the UK. Employing over 100,000 people, it is one of the largest companies in Europe.

Recent trends in UK telecommunications, especially in mobile telecommunications and Internet traffic, have helped BT increase its turnover to over £18,233 million in 1999. Despite increased competition in the telecommunications sector, BT still looks after more than 20 million domestic UK customers and thousands of businesses.

Whilst most people will recognise BT as the main provider of domestic telephone lines and digital business lines, such as ISDN, BT is extremely successful in integrating telecom-munications and IT technologies. This means it is able to diversify its business interests across many IT areas; *Syntegra* and *Syncordia*, BT's systems integration and outsourcing businesses, are prime examples of how complex IT and telecommunications technologies can be used and managed successfully. Syncordia Solutions, for example, is the UK's largest provider of managed and outsourced network solutions and has more than 27,000 clients in 46 countries.

Career opportunities

As you might expect from a huge organisation committed to employing high-calibre people, BT can offer many exciting career prospects. It is currently attracting graduates who can use the latest computer languages, be involved in innovative multimedia and Internet services and who can analyse a business idea and create solutions for it. A few of the areas you could work in include:

■ technical specialist (sales);
■ research and development;
■ Internet and multimedia applications;
■ systems and software;
■ project management.

Sandwich placements are available, as are student skills training workshops.

Graduate recruitment

Graduates are seen as critical to the future success of BT, possessing up-to-date knowledge and skills. BT has a large annual intake of graduates, and a proportion of them will need to be IT literate. For most graduate opportunities, BT expect you to hold at least a good second class honours degree in a relevant discipline (you must also have GCSE Maths and English Language at Grade C or above – or equivalent qualifications).

Contact information

The company only recruits through its careers Web site – you cannot apply on paper. If you do not have access to the

Internet, try your local library or cybercafé (some branches of Tesco provide Internet access facilities). Further details are available on BT's Web site: www.bt.com/recruitment/graduate. BT Recruitment helpdesk: (0800) 671 098.

Company profile: Cisco Systems

Cisco Systems is a major supplier of networking solutions for the Internet. Cisco's products connect people, computers and networks, allowing people to access or transfer information without regard to differences in time, place or type of computer system. Cisco serves customers in three target markets:

▌ Enterprises – large organisations with complex networking needs, usually spanning multiple locations and types of computer systems. Enterprise customers include corporations, government agencies, utilities and educational institutions.

▌ Service providers – companies that provide information services, including telecommunication carriers, Internet Service Providers, cable companies, and wireless communication providers.

▌ Small/medium business – companies with a need for data networks of their own, as well as connection to the Internet and/or to business partners.

Cisco sells its products in approximately 115 countries through a direct sales force, distributors, value-added resellers and system integrators. Cisco has headquarters in San Jose, US, as well more than 225 sales and support offices in 75 countries. Cisco develops its products and solutions around widely accepted industry standards, and in some cases, these technologies have become industry standards themselves.

Career opportunities
In the UK, Cisco has offices in London, Stockley Park (near Heathrow), Manchester, Bellshill (Scotland), Edinburgh and

Dublin. Recent recruitment campaigns at Cisco have advertised the following opportunities:

▌ systems engineers;
▌ customer support engineers;
▌ project managers;
▌ software developers.

Starting at Cisco, you can expect to enjoy a significant degree of responsibility within months. As well as technical training, you will be assigned a mentor, encouraged to pursue your individual needs and interests and steered toward Cisco's highly-respected professional qualifications up to the CCIE level (Cisco Certified Internetworking Expert).

Graduate recruitment
Cisco has a graduate recruitment team, which manages recruitment throughout the UK and the rest of Europe. Cisco, like many large IT employers, has a graduate recruitment programme. For graduate opportunities you will be expected to have a 2:1 degree or above in an IT subject or a related discipline. Whilst this is not always necessary, you must have a proven interest in networking and telecommunications.

Contact information
More information on graduate opportunities at Cisco can be found on their graduate recruitment Web-site at www.cisco-graduate-recruit.com. Alternatively contact the Graduate Recruitment Team on (020) 8756 8650 or at Cisco's UK Headquarters:

Cisco Systems
3 & 4 The Square
Stockley Park
Uxbridge
Middlesex, UB11 1BN
Tel: (020) 8756 8000

Internet Service Providers

Any business operating a Web-site, such as a high street shop, a train company or a government department, must use telecommunications services to allow customers to access their information and services. Internet Service Providers (ISPs) provide such a service by allowing other companies and individuals access to their network for their own purposes, such as hosting a Website and using electronic mail. In many cases, the ISP will also provide systems integration, e-commerce, security, software development and database management services to the customer, allowing them to deploy business systems and services on the Internet safely and profitably.

Company profile: World Online UK

World Online is an Internet Service Provider, which launched in the UK in September 1999. As a company, World Online is a relative newcomer to the world of IT and telecommunications, being founded in 1996 by Dutch entrepreneur Nina Brink.

It operates in 15 European countries and already has over 1.2 million users and over 30,000 business clients.

In the UK, World Online provides a number of Internet access products, portals and e-commerce services. As you might expect, it also has a number of strategic alliances with companies such as Reuters, Oracle and Netscape. Its main competition for Internet-related business within the UK comes from Freeserve and AOL (the two top ISPs in the UK).

As a new Internet startup company, World Online has a modern approach to IT and business, recognising the need to discuss what needs to be done and how best to do it. Its technical team has some astute minds – and they need to be; the pace of online business is incredibly fast. All its employees are given IT training from day one to understand their role within the business. The work is hard, but with stock options and preparations for flotation on the stock market, the rewards could be enormous

Personal profile: Amir Hashmi

Position: IT development manager
Age: 23
Salary: £30,000+
Average day: 9am–8.30pm (often working at home afterwards)
Background: Moved from BOL, an online book company
Opinion: The first six months of an Internet start-up are really hectic because this is when we're building everything. After the first six months, things slow down a bit, but it is still hectic. You have to use your initiative and work under huge amounts of pressure.

Personal profile: Altaf Suleman

Position: IT systems support engineer
Age: 30
Salary: £25,000–£32,000
Average day: 8.30am–6.30pm
Background: Worked with Merrill Lynch and Deutsche Bank supporting traders and bankers
Opinion: If you are thinking about joining a start-up you need to look at how the company is marketing itself. How many customers does it have and how fast are the numbers growing? Also keep an eye out for the competition; because once you join, you need to know when to jump ship.

Further information
Further information on World Online can be found on its Web site: www.worldonline.co.uk.

Communication security companies

If you provide the means to trade with millions of people globally every day of the year, you must ensure people using the Internet (especially when dealing with highly sensitive commercial or financial information) can do so with the knowledge that the information they are transferring will not get into the wrong hands. It is an awesome responsibility. Whilst this very page was drafted for publication, yet another disturbing security breach was already making front-page news. In this instance (and by no means the only one), a leading UK Internet bank was hacked into, causing thousands of pounds of losses.

Computer security in general is a sensitive issue for governments and private industry alike. As the Director of Security for a leading international organisation recently stated, 'Security is not an audit process or technical discipline, but a fundamental part of everything we do and the way we think.'

With the growth in Internet-based services, the security and integrity of computer networks and systems is becoming a 'hot' skill. Those with key skills can earn huge sums of money in consultancy – with the knowledge that they are saving their clients thousands if not millions, by preventing electronic theft and computer fraud. In the case of financial companies operating online banking and insurance services in particular, whilst their main computing systems are protected against Internet hackers, they cannot be sure how secure customers' PCs are when they are connected to their systems. If the customer of an online bank has a 'Trojan horse' virus on their PC, their personal details could end up being sent to another recipient (the hacker usually) via the bank's system. The question of financial liability (which could be staggering) is then a key issue.

Computer security is a fast-moving field, and no sooner has a security measure been announced, than there will be someone out there trying to crack it – either for a bit of fun, or for more damaging purposes. If you remember the enormous coverage given to the 'Melissa' virus, which brought down government computer systems as well as commercial systems. However, as soon as it was contained, most of the IT-literate world was affected by the 'I love you' virus, which had an equally disastrous effect on IT systems all over the world.

Company profile:
Government Communications Headquarters (GCHQ)

In business, knowledge is power. For GCHQ it's vastly more important. Knowledge ensures our nation's security, economic well-being and protection against serious crime. As you might expect, GCHQ employs some of the most highly-skilled analysts within the IT and telecommunications industries.

Career opportunities

In order for GCHQ to provide the highest quality intelligence and communications security services, it always has requirements for IT developers, computer scientists and IT specialists. In addition, fast-track graduate trainee project manager programmes are available.

General computing and IT

Opportunities include: system design, software development and support, high-speed networks, database management systems, major IT systems acquisition, advanced computer technologies or new approaches to computer security.

Computer scientists and IT specialists

Playing a vital role in providing intelligence and communications security, you can expect to work with some of the country's leading computer scientists on research and development projects. Typical projects include: signal processing, radio and satellite systems, supercomputers and high-speed networks.

Fast-track technical programmes

GCHQ offers two schemes accredited by the Institute of Electrical Engineers and the British Computer Society (IEE/BCS). The graduate trainee project manager programme is designed to help you to develop the skills you will need to manage the many technical projects undertaken by GCHQ. The graduate technologist programme concentrates on developing your knowledge and skills in your chosen applied technology field. The programme will ultimately enable you to become a Senior Engineer, dealing with some of GCHQ's biggest technical challenges.

Entry requirements

For most opportunities within GCHQ you will need a degree (2:2 or higher in an IT related subject) or be of graduate calibre with four years' IT experience. An HND/HNC (or equivalent) in an IT related subject plus two years' work experience will also be considered. You will also need to display good logical and problem-solving skills and be a good team worker. To join the graduate fast-track programmes you should have a 2:1 honours degree in a relevant engineering/scientific or IT-related discipline.

Salary

Starting salaries presently range from £16,221 to £23,256, depending on experience and qualifications. You'll get an annual review every October. Performance-related pay enables those who perform to a consistently high standard to benefit accordingly. The graduate fast-track programmes have a starting salary ranging from £17,948 to £23,256, depending on experience and qualifications.

Student sponsorship

GCHQ provides two technical student sponsorship schemes for undergraduates:

Student Scientist Engineer Scheme

The Student Scientist Engineer Scheme (SSE) provides sponsorship throughout your degree course, with an annual bursary and useful work experience. Main features include:

- annual summer work experience of at least nine weeks;
- optional one-year work experience and training placement;
- annual £1,500 bursary;
- annual £200 book grant;
- mentor assigned throughout SSE programme.

83

On successful completion of degree, features include an automatic consideration for a permanent post and an additional bursary of £300 a year of sponsored study, held over.

Sponsored Engineer and Scientist Scheme

The Sponsored Engineer and Scientist Scheme (SES) provides:

- summer work experience placement before final year;
- £1500 bursary for final year;
- assistance with final year project.

On successful completion of degree:

- two-year contract as a mainstream technologist;
- £300 grant;
- automatic consideration for permanent post.

What you need

The SSE scheme requires you to be about to start your final year of A levels (ie making your UCAS choices), or be currently in the first year of an honours degree in a relevant engineering/ scientific or IT related discipline (eg Electronics, Electronic Engineering, Communications, Computing, Information Technology, Physics etc). For the SES scheme you need to be about to start or in the early stages of your penultimate year. Both schemes can lead to the offer of a permanent position.

Contact information

The GCHQ recruitment team can be contacted on (01242) 232912 or (01242) 232913, Monday–Friday 8.30am–4.30pm. Alternatively, e-mail them at recruitment.gchq@dial.pipex.com.

Company profile: Internet Security Systems (ISS)

ISS is a specialist developer of electronic security management solutions. Formed in 1992, it provides software and services for enabling secure e-commerce. In particular, ISS offers solutions that reduce the risk of compromised digital assets;

prevent business disruptions and protect the integrity, availability and privacy of online data and operating systems.

Company profile: VeriSign

VeriSign is probably the most well-known issuer of digital certificates on the Web, being used by many of the leading software vendors. Digital security is now big business and VeriSign, along with rivals such as Entrust Technologies, develops software to secure online transactions using Public Key Infrastructure (PKI) technology as companies begin to conduct far more complex transactions over the Internet. PKI systems issue and manage digital certificates that provide electronic IDs for users of online systems.

Further information

General telecommunications

The telecommunications industry is an extremely fast-moving and exciting area. All the standard IT-related publications are worth reading; they all have major sections on telecommunications and networking. Additionally, you might want to look at the following Web sites that track and discuss the major issues affecting the industry:

www.telecoms-mag.com
www.tmav.com

WAP/WML

The WAP Forum provides training information. Contact them via their Web site: www.wapforum.org.

Information on WAP/WML can be found at http://wap.colorline.no/wap-faq.

General IT security sites

www.itsec.gov.uk

Specific Internet security Web sites

www.cert.org
(Computer Emergency Response Team formed by US Defense Advanced Research Projects Agency (DARPA) in 1988)

www.advisor.com/wHome.nsf/w/MISmain
(homepage for Internet Security magazine)

www.webreference.com/internet/security.html
(useful security links and contacts)

www.hi-media.co.uk/uk_security
(the UK Internet Security Directory)

Top jobs within networking and telecommunications

The network engineer
Installing, configuring and supporting these networks places huge demands on skilled network engineers, especially (as often is the case with top IT jobs) as demand easily outstrips supply. Over the last 10 years, networks have become extremely complex entities, often supporting thousands of users worldwide every day of the year. Similarly, computer networks no longer just transfer simple data streams between one location and the next. Today's digital high-speed networks (the information superhighway), carry real-time voice, music, images and video to thousands of people every day using satellite technology for worldwide coverage.

Key tasks and skills
Table 4.2 summarises the key tasks and skills for a network engineer.

The working environment
Do not be mistaken, the 1980s image of the network engineer doing nothing more than fitting network cards to PCs and

Table 4.2 Key tasks and skills for a network engineer

Key Tasks	Essential Skills	Desirable Skills
PLANNING • designing network connectivity either locally, nationally or globally; • evaluating appropriate network hardware and software; • designing traditional client server and 'thin'-client server networks.	• ability to create and understand network topology diagrams; • experience of at least one major networking vendor's equipment; • experience of networking configuration software such as Microsoft or Novell.	• understanding general issues and technologies in telecommunications; • knowledge of networking protocols such as TCP/IP, ATM and Frame Relay.
COMMUNICATION • understanding users' network requirements (such as file and printer sharing); • working closely with technical architects in planning the overall system architecture; • working closely with third party network hardware and software vendors.	• explaining often technical and complex issues in an understandable manner; • presenting network strategies and configurations to senior management.	• negotiating and influencing skills; • report writing.
IMPLEMENTING • installing and implementing networks on time and with as little disruption to the business as possible; • installing network software tools.	• project management skills; • specific vendor qualifications for network hardware and software.	• awareness of other issues related to networking, such as the project lifecycle, testing and post-implementation support.
PROBLEM SOLVING • diagnosing and solving network related issues (hardware and software issues).	• specific knowledge of network hardware and software.	• knowledge of fault diagnosis software.

rummaging around under-floor voids routing network cables has no place in today's information society. If the truth be known, sorting out the cabling (unfortunately, there are some things that you still need, even in the 21st century) is probably the easiest part of the job – guaranteeing sub-second response times for real-time television broadcasting over the Internet is a bit harder! Network engineers are responsible for the design, development and support of a variety of networking hardware (such as fibre-optic systems, modems and routing devices) and software (such as network traffic monitors, GUI-based network topology mapping systems and network protocol emulation software).

Salary

Junior network engineers, with a minimum of 12 months' experience, can expect to earn around £20,000, rising to £30,000 with more experience (depending on location). Senior network engineers performing a support role can expect to earn between £25,000 and £35,000, especially if they possess skills that remain in demand, such as Cisco.

Senior network architects, responsible for network design, testing and installation, can expect much higher salaries. Dependent on location, an experienced network architect can expect to earn anything from £60,000 upwards.

In response to the huge demand for skilled network engineers, many IT practitioners with networking skills are now turning to the freelance market. Roughly speaking, a freelance network engineer working as a network architect/consultant can expect to earn around £2,500 a week. For more details of contract work, refer to Chapter 7.

Entry, training and career development

Network engineers will usually have a degree in a specific IT discipline or a broader discipline such as electronic engineering. Knowledge of networking hardware and software is key to this role, and so any graduate or postgraduate options that include networking and communication systems (especially high-speed digital communications) are extremely useful. Specific postgraduate courses are available: such as Telecommunications and Information Systems; Data Communications and Computer Networks.

For those graduates who may not feel their qualification provides them with specific networking skills, there are a number of accredited training programmes offered by all the major training organisations and network vendors. The two most popular qualifications are Novell's Certified Netware Engineer scheme and Microsoft's Certified Systems Engineer scheme (details of both of these schemes can be found in Chapter 12). There are, of course, many other training programmes available to those wanting a top job in networking; the training schemes offered by Cisco (a leading network hardware vendor) are extremely popular amongst some IT companies, as are more general networking skills, such as TCP/IP and UNIX.

The IT network security consultant

An IT network security consultant will often work alone or in a very small team, working closely with the customer. It is very much an analysis role, trying to understand and assess the potential threats to their system. As the recipient of sensitive company information (especially if working for a government agency) you may well be exposed to formal security vetting procedures as part of the recruitment process and regular security checks during your assignment.

With access to the Internet now possible to anyone with a PC, modem and browser software, commercial security is now a big issue. There have already been a number of well-publicised articles highlighting how hackers have accessed commercially sensitive and financial information on Web sites such as Amazon.com, CNN Interactive and the online auction-site eBay. Security breaches like these only strengthen public perception that hackers are malicious individuals who gain satisfaction by causing untold damage at the expense of others. Just before you start wondering why I might be suggesting you could find a top job in IT as a computer system hacker, there are hackers who work for the benefit of the IT world. These IT security consultants are 'ethical hackers', as they legitimately try to penetrate 'secure' systems on behalf of a business client (or a government agency) to test how vulnerable their site or application is to external threats.

Key tasks and skills

A network security consultant will often need to combine strong technical skills with a certain flair for investigation and commercial counter-terrorism. Table 4.3 summarises the key tasks and skills for an IT network security consultant.

Table 4.3 Key tasks and skills for an IT network security consultant

Key Tasks	Essential Skills	Desirable Skills
ANALYTICAL • performing security audits of IT systems and networks (eg company Web sites); • performing penetration tests; • identifying security requirements.	• UNIX, NT and TCP/IP communications; • Public Key Infrastructure (PKI); • knowledge of firewall technologies; • the ability to apply security techniques to business problems; • secure network design (including firewalls and routers); • authentication and authorisation models.	• port-scanning tools (eg Nmap) and monitoring tools (eg Spynet); • vulnerability assessment software; • knowledge of vendor-specific security hardware and software; • cryptographic tools, techniques and technologies.
COMMUNICATION • preparing and presenting security policies for clients; • discussing specific security needs; • presenting security recommendations to management.	• clear written and verbal skills; • understanding commercial requirements and assessing commercial risks.	• report writing; • presentation skills; • risk management.
MANAGING • managing software developers to ensure security is integrated into business systems.	• the software development lifecycle; • experience of building security into the application process; • the law pertaining to computers, such as the Computer Misuse Act and Data Protection Act.	• knowledge of national and international security standards.

The working environment
An Internet security consultant will often work alone, assessing the level of threat to a company's Web-based IT systems. Working in this field requires a lot of patience – it is very much a battle of wills, helped of course by the use of fairly sophisticated software. A typical assignment for an Internet security consultant will be to perform a series of penetration tests (hacking into a system with the owner's permission) to determine how well the client's IT security systems identify and prevent unauthorised access. Assignments will usually conclude with a report of findings and recommendations to the client.

Salary
Graduates with a broad range of IT skills can expect to earn somewhere in the region of £20,000–£25,000 whilst they are receiving specialist training. An experienced IT security specialist can earn in the region of £35,000 in the public sector, but considerably more if working for a private security consultancy organisation.

Entry, training and career development
Typically, a science-based degree is a minimum for most companies recruiting IT security specialists. Degrees in computing/computer science, mathematics, physics, electronics and communications would be the most relevant. For those graduates or experienced professionals seeking a career move, relevant scientific or IT-based experience would be required (usually in the region of four years' worth).

Matthew _is a Senior Consultant working for a specialist security company._

Like a lot of other people my age (31), my original career aspirations did not include information technology (I have a degree in Electronic Engineering). However, for many reasons I became involved in IT and ended up as an IT manager responsible for security issues. I thought it was a bit ironic really, as the only experience I had of IT security issues was when I tried to hack into the university's computer system during my degree! As an IT security manager I picked up a lot of my knowledge of hacking and how to prevent it. Most of this information I obtained by talking to other people in similar roles at conferences and seminars, but I did also talk to hackers themselves, that is 'real' hackers as well as 'ethical' hackers like me. Unfortunately, I was made redundant from this role after 18 months. I had no idea what to do, until I bumped into a friend of mine who worked in the sales department of an IT security company. The rest, as they say, is history!

5 *End-user computing*

IT is now used in practically every business organisation worldwide. How it is used varies enormously – the local corner shop might possess a single computer terminal to process national lottery tickets whereas a large multinational company might invest millions in the latest IT and global communication systems so it can transfer information worldwide. Both types of organisation, however, are using IT for the same reason; to improve their business either by increasing revenue or by improving existing business functions. These organisations, the *users* of IT, form an important part of the IT community; they are the people who will decide whether or not to use the latest technology available. If they choose not to use such technology, preferring to stay with existing 'tried and tested' systems, many IT vendors risk losing vital sales.

Major IT users

Banking and finance

Since the introduction of the cash machine (or automatic teller machine), the banking and finance sector has probably seen the greatest level of change since the introduction of IT. By using the Internet to provide online banking and share-dealing services, this sector more than ever is now completely dependent on computing and IT. One major high street bank alone, the National Westminster, in 1998 had more than 800 full-time and 300 part-time IT staff!

Retail
Many traditional forms of trading, such as shopping at the local supermarket, are now undergoing many changes. IT not only

allows the supermarkets to operate more efficiently (and therefore make greater profits), but has also given them the capability to trade using new technologies such as the Internet and interactive TV.

Food is not the only retail sector to benefit from new technology. During 1999, Vauxhall became the first car manufacturer in the world to sell its cars on the Internet. Woolworth's, the major high street department store, recently completed a successful trial of interactive TV, where customers using specially configured digital TV sets accessed the store's 'shopping directory' and ordered goods from the comfort of their own home. What used to be thought of as 'shopping of the future' is readily available today.

Travel

Reservation systems, ticketing systems and in-flight services are just a few of the main types of business applications used within the travel industry. They all require huge computer systems and databases to store customer and flight information from travel agencies and airline companies situated all over the world. The travel industry has been quick to benefit from the Internet – many airline companies such as British Airways, Lufthansa, American Airlines and British Midland all have Web sites that provide online booking services for their passengers.

Computing in the public sector

The perception of working in the public sector (in schools, hospitals and local government for instance) has not always been a good one. Public sector IT, whilst having avoided many of the problems associated with the sector (such as the lack of investment and stifling bureaucracy), has experienced its own challenges, most notably those caused by *outsourcing* the IT department to another company. Now, a few years later, many of the outsourcing deals have not been as successful as hoped, with the result of either bringing back the IT department 'in-house' or by changing the way the outsourcing is managed to ensure real benefits are gained. Much of the old bureaucracy has gone, many working practices have changed and there is a new 'openness' within the sector as a whole.

For the newcomer to IT, the public sector now offers good opportunities for career development up to the highest levels of office. Not only do public sector IT staff tend to stay longer in their jobs than their counterparts in private industry, they also feel they make a greater social contribution as well. Unfortunately, some ridiculous comparisons are made between IT staff working within the public and private sectors, mainly in the areas of pay and promotion. Whilst IT managers cannot always reward staff with huge bonuses in the public sector, many public sector IT staff did receive bonuses for critical millennium work during 1999 – many being well over £2,000.

Contrary to popular belief that the public sector cannot offer a rewarding IT career, it might surprise you to know that the public sector in the UK runs some of the largest and most complex IT projects in Europe. The National Health Service alone is pioneering new technology all the time, allowing the sharing of medical records and clinical data in the quest for greater benefits. Local authorities, which employ over 18,000 IT staff in the UK, use huge IT systems to collect Council Tax and distribute housing benefit. Whilst these systems are generally not 'leading edge' in the sense they do not extend our boundaries of knowledge in IT, they are huge, complex and require the skills of many IT professionals to design, build and support.

Throughout the UK and Europe, governments are already developing IT strategies and training programmes to make use of IT in a way that has never happened before. Traditional forms of communication will gradually be replaced with new technologies. The humble domestic TV set will be used to deliver important forms and information to citizens throughout the country. In fact, it won't be long before a visit to your local post office will reveal a network of Internet-capable PCs rather than a weighing machine and a cash register.

Company profile: The Post Office

The Post Office is one of the biggest (and earliest) users of IT in the UK and makes use of a very wide range of computing technologies and methods. It has a central IT unit (with about 1,000 people based in Farnborough, Hants, and Chesterfield, Derbyshire), which provides support and services across the Post Office businesses, and there are many more people working on computerised systems within those businesses.

Degree students (not necessarily on computing or IT courses) can apply for a limited number of places with the Post Office during or shortly after their last year. Those selected are put through a carefully designed programme of training courses and six-month placements in different departments, with the intention of preparing them to become the senior specialists and managers of the future.

The other group of IT people joining the Post Office are those who have already gained some knowledge and experience elsewhere. With the size and range of IT activities in the Post Office, there is a steady demand for new people and promotion can be very fast for the right people. Salary arrangements and other benefits for IT people have to be more flexible than is usual in large organisations to ensure that the Post Office can compete successfully in the very busy and fast-moving IT job market.

Contact information
Further information may be obtained from:

The Post Office
IT Services
Concept 2000
250 Farnborough Road
Farnborough
Hants GU14 7LU
Tel: (01252) 528000

6 Working in hardware design and manufacturing

Despite the boom in software, computer hardware is still a substantial area within the IT industry. In 1993, the European computer market was estimated at £130 billion and growing. One-third of this total was spent with the hardware manufacturers.

During the early days of computing, the computer industry was dominated by a few huge companies (such as IBM and ICL) who were, in fact, hardware suppliers. The hardware market has changed significantly since then, and the IT industry has adopted a more 'open' approach. Customers are no longer forced to buy their computer hardware and software from the same manufacturer – they can go to any number of IT vendors. As a result, many hardware manufacturers now employ 'open' standards for chip design, computer interfaces and networking, allowing them to integrate their equipment with equipment from other manufacturers.

Key manufacturers

Computers, regardless of shape, size or cost, rely upon silicon chips for their operation. As the demand for even more powerful computers increases, so too will the need for specialists capable of designing and manufacturing them. Almost 90 per cent of the high-performance chips found within large midrange and mainframe computers are produced by Japanese-owned companies, such as Fujitsu and Mitsubishi, whilst the circuits found within most PCs are produced largely by American manufacturers such as Intel and Motorola.

It is worth remembering that careers in computer system manufacture involve a great deal more than just designing and testing integrated circuits. All computer systems are worthless unless there is some means of entering data into them and retrieving information from them. Every computer system, therefore, requires input and output devices, called peripherals, which include printers, display screens and storage devices (disks and tapes). There may also be a range of networking and telecommunication equipment attached to the computer to allow information to be routed to another computer anywhere in the world. Computer peripherals are manufactured throughout the world, including the UK and the rest of Europe.

Career prospects

Computer hardware manufacturers can offer many highly skilled careers, which cover every aspect of the manufacturing process from design to distribution and support. Disk storage technology in particular is growing at an incredible rate, trying to satisfy the demands placed on companies as a result of the Internet revolution.

Bear in mind, though, working for a hardware manufacturer does not necessarily mean the only career options available to you are based around manufacture and support – consultancy roles are always in demand with hardware vendors. IT professionals in these roles will be required to offer advice to IT organisations that require the vendor's technology. With any major hardware installation, integration and change management are key areas where professional advice may be needed.

Qualifications

If you want to enter the area of computer manufacture such as microprocessor design and digital electronic technology at a professional level, you will normally require a degree in IT, electronics or maths. Many of the larger computer manufacturers such as IBM, Hewlett-Packard and Sun Microsystems have extremely good graduate training programmes, and recruit graduates with degrees in any discipline.

Company profile: IBM UK

IBM UK is a subsidiary of the IBM Corporation, which is one of the world's largest suppliers of information technology hardware, software solutions and services. IBM is truly a worldwide IT company, providing solutions to customers in over 130 countries. Within the UK, IBM has sites at more than 25 locations, including Basingstoke, Bedfont Lakes, Greenock, Hursley, London, Portsmouth, Manchester and Warwick. IBM's main activities include:

- manufacturing;
- development and support for computer software and hardware;
- software and consultancy services;
- Internet development and electronic trading services.

All the manufacturing carried out by IBM in the UK is performed at their Greenock site in Scotland. IBM employs more than 3,000 people at this site in a wide variety of manufacturing and technical roles ranging from high-volume assembly to IT management. IBM Greenock is responsible for the development, manufacture and support of PCs for the European, Middle Eastern and African markets, and is the only site within IBM worldwide where design, manufacture and support are completely integrated. Already they employ over 250 overseas staff who manage the customer's order from manufacture to delivery. This is carried out for 76 countries in 17 different languages. One of the most popular IBM products, the award-winning IBM ThinkPad, is manufactured entirely at Greenock.

Qualifications required

IBM accepts graduates from many disciplines, ranging from scientific and computing areas to the arts. As you would expect from a company with such a wide range of career options, IBM can offer employment at all levels; and for the more technical positions, it welcomes graduates with Master's degrees. Having operations throughout the world, it is particularly keen to recruit IT professionals with language skills as well as technical skills. IBM regularly advertises at recruitment fairs and exhibitions throughout the year.

Contact information
Available from:

Recruitment Services
PO Box 41
North Harbour
Portsmouth
Hants PO6 3AU

Company profile: Intel Ireland Ltd

Intel Ireland is a subsidiary of the massive Intel Corporation, one of the market leaders in microprocessor design and manufacture. It is one of the largest IT companies to invest in Ireland, with over $1 billion invested in its Ireland operation by the end of 1995.

Intel's manufacturing complex in County Kildare is the company's sole manufacturing centre for Europe, with four factories on-site. The company directly employs over 2,800 people, with another 800 people being employed on-site by other service companies. Intel's main activities include:

▌ manufacture of semi-conductor products (eg Pentium processor);
▌ manufacture of PC motherboards;
▌ manufacture of PCs and servers for leading computer vendors;
▌ PC maintenance and repair.

Qualifications required
Over one-third of Intel employees are graduates. However, due to the wide-ranging skills used within the company, graduates are recruited from many disciplines, such as electronic engineering, mechanical engineering, computer

science and information technology. As you would expect from a company whose operations are widespread, Intel can offer employment at all levels within the company; as a minimum, it recruits entry-level employees with five passes on their Leaving Certificate (the Irish equivalent of A-levels).

Intel readily accepts 'on-spec' CVs for current and future positions – these are scanned electronically and stored on their recruitment database. Should a vacancy exist (Intel are currently recruiting heavily) the database is searched and a short-list drawn up.

Contact information
This may be obtained from:

Personnel Department
Collinstown Industrial Park
Leixlip
County Kildare
Ireland
Tel: (00 353) 1 606 7000

Freelance contracting

Despite changes in UK tax law regarding self-employed contract staff (the infamous IR35 ruling), contracting can still be a lucrative and rewarding career. All of the major reports on employment opportunities commissioned predict that there will be a gradual rise in the number of contract IT vacancies. Immediately after the millennium date change, many companies shed large numbers of contractor staff, many of whom were on incredible hourly rates (the so-called 'Cobol-millionaires'), creating a significant depression in the contract market. Now that confidence and stability in IT systems has been restored, many company budgets, having being frozen approaching the new millennium, have now been approved for new IT projects.

As an IT graduate, or experienced professional with specific IT skills, the thought of contracting might appeal to you, but it is important to weigh up the pros and cons of entering the contract market before you make your decision. Is it absolutely essential to identify what skills are in demand out in the freelance world? Yes, there is a skills shortage, but you must still be a marketable proposition if you are to compete for the best contracts where competition is rife. The SSP survey mentioned in Chapter 1 is a very worthwhile place to start.

As with any job, what is important is getting your first steps on the ladder. Contracting is no different, and in some ways slightly harder, if only because of the legal and financial considerations. Potential contractors come from two main sources: ambitious but relatively inexperienced people coming straight out of university and those with lots of skills and experience who are currently employed but not necessarily working for an IT company (people like you, in other words). Whatever category you fall into, the good news is that there is a multitude of Web sites, agencies and other sources of information you can use to help you on your way.

How to win your first contract

To find that first contract, most potential contractors will normally need to enlist the help of an agency that specialises in the IT contracts market. Don't believe all you read about recruitment agencies; they know the market and most will offer expert advice on how to work successfully within it. Agencies are the middle-men between their clients (you) and the organisations requiring short or long-term contract staff. It is possible for a contractor to obtain work directly from a client (through networking maybe), but it is unusual for a first-time contractor to do so.

To find your dream job in IT, planning and preparation are vital. Contracting is no different. It is vital to scan the main IT publications and Web sites that feature contract jobs. These will give you an idea of the types of skill in demand and the geographical areas where skills are concentrated. Do not expect to see rates of pay given in contract advertisements; they must be negotiated with the agency (average rates of pay for popular contracts are given later in this chapter).

Top tips on winning an IT contract

- Always send a good covering letter with your application. Use it to pick up points that modesty or space prevents you from putting on your CV.
- Provide two referees on your CV, including their official titles, addresses and telephone numbers.
- Learn as much as you can about the company you are considering contracting for (such as size, products, locations, style and, crucially, its reputation as an employer (you don't have many rights as a contractor)).
- Many agencies, especially those recruiting for e-commerce skills, prefer people with practical experience. If you are serious about becoming a contractor, but not just yet, use your time well and gain at least a year's experience with a large organisation first.

▌ If you're interested in working for a specific company, find out if it has a preferred supplier agency so you know who to register with.

▌ The first contract is the most important one. Determine your own objectives for contracting and then assess the offers you get against them.

▌ If you are contracting for the first time, ensure your contract carries a fair notice period – four weeks either way is acceptable.

▌ Never tell an agency where you have had interviews or who you are potentially going to have an interview with – they may send in their own candidate.

Choosing a suitable agency

Unfortunately, within the recruitment industry (and not just the IT recruitment industry), there are good contract agencies and there are bad contract agencies. The good ones will be in regular contact with you, providing up-to-date information on skills and employers; tax law and general business advice; the bad ones will leave you very much in the dark whilst earning a nice commission when they do eventually arrange your first contract.

To help you in your quest, industry bodies such as the Recruitment and Employment Confederation (REC) can prove invaluable. An agency that sports the REC logo is your assurance that the company works to a recognised Code of Good Recruitment Practice. Recruitment Consultants and Managers who are individual members of the REC are committed professionals who have demonstrated a level of competence and experience. You can use the services of the REC to help you locate a good agency in your local area. A list of recommended contract agencies is shown in Table 7.1.

Owing to the lack of skills in the industry, many agencies will take you on if you show the right qualities at the interview. It is in this situation where the good recruitment consultants can start to work their magic. Many clients will listen to a good recruitment consultant who says, 'I know a great guy/girl who has been developing Web sites from his/her bedroom – and here are the URLs.' They may be prepared to see him or her, whereas once upon a time they would have wanted someone with experience from a top dot.com company.

Table 7.1 Recommended contract agencies

Name	Contact Number	Web Site Address
Best	(020) 7300 9000	www.best-international.com
Capital Software	(01444) 235577	www.capital-software.com
Computer Futures	(020) 7446 6666	www.compfutures.com
Computer People	(020) 7440 2000	www.computerpeople.co.uk
Harvey Nash	(020) 7333 0033	www.harveynash.com
Pendragon Recruitment	(01454) 411219	www.pendragon-recruitment.co.uk
Parity Resources	(01442) 240761	www.parity-resources.com
Rullion	(0161) 941 5335	www.rullion.co.uk

Working abroad

With many of the traditional barriers to employment abroad now removed, especially within the European Union, the IT skills shortage is now providing an ideal opportunity for people to win contracts throughout Europe and the US. Such is the demand for skilled IT professionals abroad, winning a contract to work abroad is now almost as simple as winning a contract to work in the UK. Many top IT recruitment agencies now either specialise in international contracts or at least have an international recruitment team. For instance, Computer Futures has offices in Belgium, Dublin and the Netherlands. Contact details for these offices are:

Belgium Tel: +32 2 645 3300; e-mail: permanent@compfutures.be
Dublin Tel: +353 1 661 7666; e-mail: permanent@compfutures.ie
Netherlands Tel: +31 20 522 1717; e-mail: nl@compfutures.com

Useful recruitment sources

Traditional IT publications
For anyone wanting to be a contractor, all the major IT publications such as *Computing* and *Computer Weekly* have numerous

105

adverts for contract vacancies and articles relating to the world of contracting in general. However, *Freelance Informer* is widely regarded by many in the contract market as *the* magazine to buy if you are considering contracting at any level. In any case, it is worth reading all these publications to get a feel for the types of contract and the overall state of the contract market.

Web-based recruitment

The Internet is beginning to play an important role in helping people find their first IT contract. By accessing some of the many relevant Web sites, you can not only research suitable recruitment agencies, you can also research potential employers too. Whilst it is always a good idea for first-timers to use a specialist contract agency, through the power of the Internet, potential contractors can now apply directly to vacancies submitted by clients. The Web site, www.hy-phen.com, allows contractors to bid for how much they will charge for a specific requirement; and allows the client to choose the best contractor based on their skills, rate and availability. Another good Web site is www.ukitcontractors.com, a direct recruitment site that lets clients advertise their IT vacancies both for contract and permanent positions.

Working as a contractor

Most contractors work for themselves in the sense that they own their own limited company, into which their salary is paid by the company they are working for. Whilst the idea of being the Managing Director of your own company may boost your ego, it does have its drawbacks. For one thing, you will have to pay National Insurance premiums both as an employee *and* an employer. You will also have to pay for any training you require (unless you can make 'an arrangement' with your employer) and lose your entitlement to company sick pay.

Contractors are required in all the major areas of IT support and development for all sorts of reasons – the main one being to source a short-term skills requirement on a major project. For this reason, most contracts are between three and six months' duration, but contracts of 12 months are now becoming more common as well.

Assessing the benefits

As with most things in life, the financial gains that can be made as a contractor come at a price. Having said that, before highlighting some of the disadvantages of contracting, it is worth remembering that most freelancers believe the pros outweigh the cons:

- no paid holidays;
- no paid sick leave (although you can take out insurance cover);
- you may need to travel long distances for the right contract;
- training is almost always at your own expense.

IR35

IR35 was the name of the press release issued by the Inland Revenue in the 1999 budget and outlines the changes to the taxation of personal services companies (otherwise known as limited companies). IR35 is now law, and whilst you should seek professional advice on IR35 before accepting a contract (from either accountancy firms or specialist recruitment agencies), the following section will at least provide you with the basics.

Contracting and IR35

Precisely how IR35 will affect you as a contractor will depend on the specific details of your contract. It will, however, affect the structure under which you can operate and the amount you can earn. The fundamental purpose of IR35 is to clamp down on tax avoidance by contractors who work via limited companies.

Before the tax changes, IT contractors could set up a limited company and appoint themselves as director and become an employee of the company. By drawing a small salary they could avoid paying huge amounts of tax and National Insurance (NI) whilst receiving large dividends from the company (free of NI). As a rough guide, whilst top earners in IT expect to be hit by the highest rate of tax (40 per cent), many contractors, especially those with good accountants could get away with paying about 9 per cent! Now that's what I call a top job!

Under IR35, this structure is likely to change. Each contract must be tested against the Schedule D self-employment rules to determine the contractor's working status – employed or self-employed. If you are deemed to be on a self-employed contract, then nothing changes; you can operate as a limited company and enjoy the benefits and dividends. If you are deemed to be 'employed' you will be treated for tax purposes as PAYE and subject to income tax and NI. Depending on individual circumstances therefore, it is estimated that contractors caught out by IR35 will see their income drop by anything from 10 per cent to 45 per cent.

On a positive note, there are many ways to avoid IR35. Contracts that are 'IR35-friendly' are being offered by many agencies as a way of helping potential contractors into the market. More importantly, there are alternative ways of operating as a business (eg as a sole-trader working directly for an IT company or becoming an employee of an agency or umbrella company), which will help avoid IR35. On average, despite IR35, a contractor can still earn around two-thirds more than they would as a permanent worker. The message to anyone considering contracting (especially for first-timers) should, I hope, be clear – seek expert opinion.

Further information

IR35 is a complicated issue, so it is advisable to seek professional advice from an accountant or contact the Inland Revenue. JSA Accountancy Services is one of the UK's specialist computer contractors' accountants. JSA has offices throughout the UK and specialises in providing accountancy services to first-time and established contractors working in the UK and abroad. It will help you set up a limited, 'umbrella' or alternative type of company depending on your requirements and advise in IR35 issues. Barry Roback, FCA, the Managing Director of JSA Accountancy Services, also works as *Freelance Informer*'s financial 'agony uncle'.

Freephone (0800) 252640 or visit JSA's Web site www.jsagroup.co.uk.

In addition, many of the following Web sites provide a good source of information on IR35-related issues:

www.inlandrevenue.gov.uk/ir35
www.engineerjob.com
www.360-group.com/ir35 (Tel: (08457) 2020360)
www.giantgroup.com

www.gradprof.co.uk
www.atsco.org
www.ir35calc.co

Rates of pay

As with permanent positions, contract rates of pay differ greatly depending on location and the nature of the skill you possess. For instance, IT graduates, straight from university with Java knowledge and a bit of work experience, can expect a rate of £45 an hour in the contract market (see Table 7.2). Graduates with telecommunications skills (such as TCP/IP or Cisco certification), depending on location, can expect anything from £45 an hour to over £75 an hour. Despite an ever more mobile population, where people are prepared to relocate to find well-paid work, there are still 'skills hotspots' in the UK, where demand for one or more skills easily outstrips supply. Regular browsing of the standard IT magazines and publications will help you identify where these hotspots are, but of course, if you are wanting that lucrative freelance opportunity you've read about you may have to travel to get it. It is not unknown for contractors earning £2000 a week in central London to live in cheap B&B accommodation during the week and travel home at weekends.

Location is important for many reasons. The cost of living and travel expenses is an obvious consideration for any contract, but the location of a contract can sometimes influence the skills that

Table 7.2 Average contract rates for popular skills

Skill	Average Hourly Contract Rate
telecommunications/certified network engineers	£45
Java	£45
data warehousing	£45
Oracle	£35
UNIX	£35
C++	£30
Visual Basic	£30

locally-based employers are looking for. In the City of London, a contractor with banking and finance skills using one of the top 10 skills in demand, such as UNIX, Oracle, NT, Java and C++, will have very little difficulty finding work. However, in the Midlands, where there is a strong engineering and manufacturing influence, a top contract may require someone with embedded programming skills, hardware chip programming or real-time programming in C.

Of course, there are many contract opportunities for the popular, general technologies all over the UK, such as Visual Basic, Microsoft Office, Oracle and C++. As a rough guide, contractors with Visual Basic or C++ can expect to earn around £30 an hour and up to £50 an hour if they also possess Microsoft networking experience or Microsoft SQL Server experience. Any experience of project management (especially if you have experience of a professional project management methodology such as PRINCE) or consultancy will be a bonus that could add a few pounds onto your hourly rate.

Further information

Relevant publications

Computing/Computer Contractor
VNU Business Publications
The Circulation Manager
VNU House
32–34 Broadwick Street
London W1A 2HG
Tel: (020) 7316 9000

Computer Weekly/Freelance Informer
Reed Business Publishing
Circulation Manager
Quadrant House
The Quadrant
Sutton
Surrey SM2 5AS
Tel: (01444) 441212
Freelance Informer helpline (01622) 778222

Useful Web sites

www.rec.uk.com
www.freelanceinformer.co.uk
www.ukitcontractors.com
www.hy-phen.com

Dave _is a freelance computer contractor._

Whilst I consider myself to be an experienced IT professional, my academic qualifications are actually in Chemistry! I have a degree and a PhD in Chemistry from Manchester University, but it was my IT work at university that enabled me to consider a career as an IT contractor.

During my research, I wrote a lot of UNIX shell scripts and C code – the university had a number of powerful UNIX servers, which we regularly used. I became a UNIX systems administrator for one of the servers in the Chemistry department. This gave me peace of mind that my programs were safe, but I also used the opportunity to develop some marketable UNIX systems administration skills!

Obviously, since then I've had to read a few books on more advanced UNIX and C topics, such as kernel programming and driver routines, but even after leaving university, I was a competent C programmer and UNIX systems administrator. I did consider joining an IT organisation at first, but at that stage, I wasn't sure what role I wanted within an IT department; what I really wanted to do was continue programming. Contracting seemed a suitable option, although I didn't really know anything about it, especially all the legal and tax implications. I found my first contract through a contract agency in _Freelance Informer_, although I'm sure I would have found an equally good agency from the advertisements in _Computing_ and _Computer Weekly_. I think I will stay with this agency for a while – they help graduates and first-time contractors by offering help and advice on legal issues and even provide computer-based training to help us keep our skills refreshed. Oh, and another thing – the money makes it all worthwhile!

---

8 Careers in multimedia

Electronic publishing

The electronic publishing industry is rapidly emerging as one of the most successful sectors within information technology. With the almost seamless transition from floppy disk to CD ROM and now to digital versatile disk (DVD), the products of this new 'multimedia' industry are now readily used both in the home and within business. For instance, over 100,000 copies of Microsoft's *Encarta* encyclopedia were sold in the UK during 1994. Whilst this industry has many key players in the UK, the production of multimedia titles at present is clearly dominated by the USA.

The multimedia industry is a big user of expensive PC-based hardware and software; and although publishing techniques have changed, the objectives are still the same – to make money by selling a quality product. To develop the product (newspapers, books, videos and so on), often specialist IT hardware and software is necessary to enable complex images to be transposed onto a wide variety of media, such as paper, CD ROM, DVD and of course, the Web.

The scope for rewarding careers in this fast-moving, demanding industry is high. IT skills are used alongside publishing skills to provide many varied roles and responsibilities. Publishing tasks will involve writing, editing, proof-reading and designwork. IT tasks will involve supporting the hardware, software and networks, writing 'in-house' software for publishing tasks or even producing encryption algorithms to protect information (such as electronic books and applications) distributed on CD ROM.

The main software packages used in the electronic publishing industry can be generally categorised as:

Desktop publishing software. Similar to a word-processor, but used for editing and controlling multiple documents, such as the sections of a newspaper or chapters in a book. One of the most popular desktop publishing packages used in the industry is *QuarkXPress*.

Photo-imaging software. Practically all of the images (pictures, photographs, diagrams for example) found in books and newspapers are now produced electronically, using digital image-editing programs and scanners. Using these publishing tools, source images (such as photographs) can be 'scanned' into the computer and edited using specialist software. This software is similar to an art or graphics package that might be used in the home, allowing parts of the image to be edited. A good example of how this is used within the electronic publishing industry can be found on the front page of the 'glossy' fashion magazines. Photographs of models (especially on close-up facial shots) are often enhanced to appear perfect for the front page of the magazine. One of the most popular imaging and graphics packages used in the industry is *Adobe Photoshop*. This is a particularly popular tool within the multimedia industry as it used by all the best Web site designers for displaying digital images on company Web sites.

Entry requirements

For best jobs in this sector you will undoubtedly need a good degree. A science-based degree such as maths, physics or IT will give you a good start, but times are changing and many companies also want art and design skills. Obviously if you are graduating from a BA Arts degree that has a significant computing content, you are probably just the type of person the multimedia companies are looking for!

Careers in multimedia are particularly suitable for established professionals who have experience of the media and publishing industry. There are many opportunities in all of the major IT publications for specialist organisations seeking design skills that can be used to design commercial Web sites for clients.

Salary

Average starting salaries can be between £15,000 and £17,000 a year. Top-level graduates (by Oxford and Cambridge standards) can expect £35,000–£40,000 straight from university. Some London publishers are even offering an £8,000 'golden handshake' for students accepting offers of employment.

—— Company profile: Pearson Publishing ——

Pearson Publishing is a small group of businesses which produce high-quality educational products and services on various forms of electronic multimedia as well as on the traditional 'printed page'. In practice, this means the company not only produces materials on 'fixed' electronic media (such as CD ROM), but also on 'online' media (such as the Web).

Specialising in information and communications technology, its emphasis is on applying new technologies to the preparation of teaching, training and marketing materials.

Career opportunities

Being one of the smaller companies in this sector (not to be confused with the huge international multimedia company, Pearson plc), it needs highly motivated and bright people who can quickly become experts in all the major areas of multimedia publishing. Whilst publishing tasks such as design, editing and proof-reading are performed, these form only a part of the whole operation. Specific IT tasks such as building networks, writing in-house software, building demonstrations and supporting all the IT hardware and software are also performed. Graduates form a large part of the team within Pearson Publishing, many are from Cambridge, although graduates from any university are welcome. Typical subjects studied have been maths, physics and computing.

Specialist Web site design companies

Large organisations normally have neither the time nor expertise to build and maintain their corporate Web sites. As more and more organisations, from the local butchers shop to international conglomerates, realise the importance of having a Web site, demand for Web site design skills has increased across the whole sector. Many of the popular high street stores in the UK use skills from specialist Web site design companies, as do many of the football clubs in the Premier League. Speed of access and ease of use are seen as critical success factors in the development of any serious Web site. Research is already showing that if a user cannot access the Web page they want within a few seconds they will lose interest and go somewhere else. A company Web site is no longer just a fancy corporate logo with a few buttons on – it is the company's electronic 'shop window', and just like a shop window, it must be pleasing to the eye whilst ensuring it attracts people in through the doors to spend money.

Computer game development

The games sector, although often overlooked, is an important part of the IT industry, both in terms of hardware and software sales. Whilst there are computers available, there will always be computer games to play on them. For many PC owners, it is the only thing they use it for. Compared to the offerings from today's computer games industry, the early *Space Invaders* arcade games now seem like child's play, but they did, however, hook a generation of children and adults onto the concept of the computer game. This fact alone suggests that the computer games industry is huge. Well, it is, and that means that there are fantastic opportunities for careers in this rapidly expanding and exciting area.

Games development is a lucrative business when a hit game is produced, but is risky due to the lengthy development period and the risks involved if the game is not successful. In recent months, however, the share prices of many of the global games developers and publishers gained over 50 per cent, helped by the interest surrounding the launch of the Sony PlayStation 2. Whilst share price in an often volatile market is no firm indicator, there is no doubt that the games industry is seen as a future goldmine, attracting the attention of many large investors. Indeed, as the graphics capabilities of the new Sony PlayStation 2 are so advanced, many gaming industry experts are predicting that game development may now require a team of 80 over 18 months to produce a game that is worthy of the PlayStation's capabilities.

According to www.GameDev.net (one of the best Web sites around for anyone interested in gaming), between 1,200 and 3,000 games are released very year. Most of these are 'first-person shooters' or real-time strategy type games, genres that any would-be games entrepreneur should avoid if possible. The demand for these types of games is easily satisfied with fantastic product offerings from the market leaders in each field; there is little or no scope for the budding games writer to break into this market.

Game console manufacturers

Computer gaming is big business and an extremely serious one too. Here's an interesting irony – many of the technologies now used within mainstream IT were introduced and developed by the games industry. The Nintendo 64, for instance, was one of the first hardware devices to take advantage of 64-bit technology.

Originally, the entertainment industry concentrated mainly on audio entertainment, but over the years it changed, developing new technologies that combined information technology with new forms of audio-visual entertainment.The Sony Corporation, with a long and successful history in the entertainment business, is a perfect example of how such changes can lead to unparalleled success. Following the huge success of their PlayStation games console, the PlayStation 2 will also represent one of the most sophisticated pieces of hardware available. Providing full Internet access, it can also play DVDs – and, it uses state-of-the-art 128-bit technology as well, all for £300.

When Microsoft's X-box is released during November 2001, it will give the games industry yet another huge boost. X-box will be more technically advanced than the Sony PlayStation 2 and, knowing Microsoft, they will invest millions of dollars marketing their latest product to ensure a successful launch.

Games software companies

Mega-selling games such as *Tomb Raider* (despite what you might think) are not the product of one company; they are, in fact, the end product from a number of companies. This is no coincidence; a lot of specialist skills are needed to produce a product that in many ways is the computer equivalent of a blockbuster Hollywood movie.

Companies such as Eidos (the company behind *Tomb Raider*) do not actually write computer games software, but provide an 'umbrella group' under which lie a number of smaller companies, specialising in areas such as marketing, advertising, distribution and research. The actual design and programming aspects in the production of computer games are normally performed by a number of small, independent software development studios that are commissioned to supply computer games by the big umbrella companies, such as Eidos.

Company profile: Codemasters

Codemasters is one of the most profitable privately-owned games companies in Europe, whilst also achieving incredible success in the US. The company was set up in 1986 and is run by David and Richard Darling (aged 33 and 31 respectively) and their father Jim, a former contact lens designer and manufacturer.

Having a history of electronics within the family (David and Richard's grandfather had an interest in electronics and taught them how to design and build numerous electronic gadgets) ensured David and Richard were both technically-minded from an early age. Still, it was only when the Commodore Pet was launched (if you can remember that far back) that they started taking an interest in computers. Their father had purchased the computer to assist him in designing contact lenses, but brought it home for weekends as part of a deal with his two sons – they programmed data into it for him on the understanding they could use it to try their hand at writing games programs. The rest, as they say, is history – the homespun business idea soon escalated into selling games on old tape formats and selling them through magazines, eventually becoming a serious games development company. Codemasters was born and one of its earliest successes was a game called *Micro Machines*, a racing game that became one of the most successful franchises in the relatively short history of computer gaming. Other titles soon followed, including: *Colin McRae Rally, TOCA* and *Brian Lara Cricket*.

Today Codemasters has a well-deserved reputation, built on concentrating solely on developing AAA-rated games (mainly for the Sony PlayStation). Game development is not cheap and any game that doesn't look like it will make the grade will be terminated in the early stages of development.

Further information

A useful source of information for anyone interested in this area would be any one of the many magazines specialising in computer games. *The Edge* is a particularly good source of information, providing details on the products, companies and career opportunities within the industry, and is read by many existing games designers and programmers.

Similarly, there is no shortage of books that cover all aspects of computer gaming. Titles such as: *Tricks of the Windows Game*; *Programming Gurus* and *Real Time Strategy Game Programming Using DirectX* are worth reading. There are a number of Web sites that also provide lots of information. A favourite is www.GameDev.net, which provides technical information and 'how-to-do-it' papers, as well as lots of links to other useful gaming Web sites. Also worth a visit is www.futuregames.net.

If you prefer to use recruitment agencies, rather than apply directly to advertisements in the many computer gaming magazines, try Datascope Recruitment. They have a huge listing of computer gaming jobs, starting at £12,000 and rising to over £40,000. Datascope Recruitment can be contacted on (020) 7580 6018 or e-mail: info@datascope.co.uk.

Top jobs within multimedia

Web site designer

One of the key stages in adopting the Internet as a trading medium is designing and building a Web site. This is not a complex task as there are many tools and packages that provide this functionality – the skill is in designing a Web site that is easily navigable, informative and visually stimulating.

Web site design requires more than just IT skills, it is almost a work of art – with a very serious message. Most commercial Web sites are designed and built by one of the major IT e-commerce consultancy companies (such as IBM, EDS and ICL) or are commissioned from a specialist Web site design company, such as Plug 1 (their Web site is www.plug1.com).

Key tasks and skills

A creative flair is as important as Web design skills using software such as Microsoft _Front Page 2000_ and Active Server Pages (ASP). With new software packages being developed all the time, you must be able to learn and use new software quickly – deadlines are very important in this role.

Entry, training and career development

A degree in an IT-related subject or an art-based subject (such as graphic design with a multimedia option) will provide most of the key skills and technologies you will need in this role. Basic and advanced Web site design courses (advertised in all the popular IT magazines) may also help if you are moving into an IT career from another profession.

Salary

Graduate Web site designers with little or no experience can expect a salary of around £18,000. With experience this can rise to over £30,000.

Tom _is **Creative Director of a Web design company.**_

My job is 90 per cent creative and 10 per cent software knowledge, which I think is the right balance. There are a lot of people in the industry who have all the right software skills but lack the creative flair – in this job it's crucial. In some ways, it is an art, as you need to understand graphic design and colour theory – basically the things that make a Web page 'work'. Having these skills means you can get a job where people ask you what you can build for them, rather than have the customer tell you (usually incorrectly) what they think the Web page should look like!

I'm excited because I'm working in e-commerce, but my job does involve me using lots of other multimedia skills, such as print design and film-making. You need to have an interest in sound and animation too, as these are the properties of a Web page that will make it attractive and attention-grabbing.

Judith *is a Web site designer.*

Graduating from a BA Honours course in Graphic Design, I hardly expected to be working in the IT industry, let alone working on some of the most exciting new developments within the industry as a whole. At face value there seems little in common with this hi-tech Internet stuff and graphic design, but when you consider the impact a well-designed and built Web site has on a potential customer, then you realise why you need someone with a good 'eye', and a bit of artistic flair is perfect for the role I'm performing.

Computer gaming

The structure of a typical computer game development studio is shown in Figure 8.1.

Games programmer

As you might expect, games programmers working for games companies develop games software from an initial idea or design. There will often be more than one programmer working in a team, with each programmer working on a separate piece of the game. Whilst games programmers today have the benefit of being able to

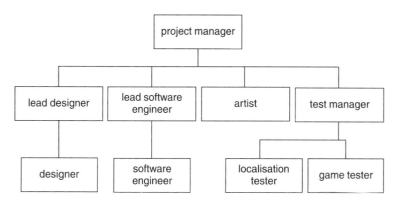

Figure 8.1   The structure of a typical computer game development studio

use sophisticated computer packages, programming skills are still extremely important.

Key tasks and skills

Unlike the world of commercial programming, there is no solution that is optimal for all applications. C is obviously a major skill in games programming as it is fast and well-suited to small applications, but it doesn't support object-oriented (OO) programming well. Its successor, C++, again another popular language throughout many areas of programming, has good OO support but is incredibly complicated. For instance, I know proficient C++ programmers who, after writing a large module in C++, still find it difficult to fully understand the program the next day, let alone a week after writing it.

On the other hand, Visual Basic and Delphi are considerably easier to learn, but are slow, non-portable (across different operating systems) and proprietary. Java is very much the skill to possess in the current Internet climate, but again, for games purposes it is slow (although it does possess many neat little features that can be used to great effect).

A key skill to track is DirectX, which is Microsoft's sophisticated set of application program interfaces (APIs). Being an integral part of Windows 98 and Windows 2000, it gives games developers a set of APIs for improved access to 3-D graphics acceleration chips and sound cards.

Entry, training and career development

As there are many standard game development and authoring tools available today, it is easy to assume that anyone can create a best-selling computer game. Not so. In a highly competitive and lucrative industry, only people with top skills (or the potential to gain top skills) will achieve success. The halcyon days of the 1980s, where you could develop a reasonably good game in your garage or garden shed and sell it for thousands of pounds to a top games company are, unfortunately, well and truly over. Modern games programming has a high mathematical emphasis and requires a disciplined, professional approach to programming, and of course, being a technical 'wizard' helps enormously too. Even if you have taught yourself how to write computer programs from a tutorial program, it does not mean you possess the right 'professional' skills to work as a programmer, such as team-working and problem-solving. For this reason, most companies will expect you to possess a good degree (upper second or first class) from a respected university. The degree should be in one of the following subjects: computing, software engineering, mathematics, physics or engineering. Of course, it is expected that you are capable of writing complex programs with little supervision.

If you do not have a maths or computing-based degree (maybe you have a PhD in Biology), and have used C extensively during your course, you must be able to demonstrate that you are an *exceptionally* good programmer who can write structured and easily maintainable code. Most games companies will want to review a sample game or routine you have written to prove your programming competence. Whatever your qualifications, you should take note of the advice given to would-be games programmers from the director of one of the top games companies: 'If you want to become a game programmer, work with a pro and learn your trade.'

Generally speaking, a good working knowledge of programming languages used for gaming, such as C, C++ and assembler, is required if you want to be a games programmer. In addition, a knowledge of artificial intelligence (AI) techniques and 3-D programming techniques would be useful.

Games artist
Key tasks and skills
A computer games artist is responsible for creating the images used within a computer game, such as characters, scenery and on-screen instructions. If the game uses complex moving images, specialist graphics packages such as 3-D Studio MAX will be used, which will save a lot of time and effort (and consequently cost).

As you might expect, to be a games artist, you will need to be a good artist rather than an IT expert. Games software companies can teach artists relevant computer skills, but they can't teach an IT expert how to be a good artist!

Entry, training and career development
A degree in Graphic Design or Art would be advantageous if you are to enter at a senior position. On-the-job training is often the normal way of progressing in this field as each games studio has its own standard techniques and graphics tools for animation and characterisation.

Games designer
Key tasks and skills
A games designer performs a number of roles, depending on the size of the development studio. If the studio employs just a few people, the games designer may well be involved in everything from designing the game (plot, characters and scenery), writing manuals and in-game text, to planning how the special visual effects and music editing tasks need to be incorporated into the game. The designer will often work closely with the Project Manager from the initial concept to the finished computer game.

Entry, training and career development
A games designer performs a crucial role in the development of a computer game and it is not an area you would move into without previous experience of the games industry. In practice, a games designer will need a number of skills such as games design, project management, scheduling and research. To help in this role, many designers use specialist computer packages that are written by the development studio (as opposed to buying an 'off-the-shelf' package).

Games tester

The games tester plays an important (and enviable) role in the development of a computer game. Testing must be methodical and thorough to ensure the game has been written to the design specification, incorporating any short-cuts, tricks and bonus screens that may have been included in the game. Whilst casual playing of the game may detect the obvious errors, only many hours testing every option and route within the game will uncover the smaller errors, which if not picked up before distribution will cause many problems.

Key tasks and skills

PC and game-playing skills are essential, but good planning skills and a methodical approach to work are equally important. To be able to test a game, the tester must first understand how the game *should* work – for instance: what should the screens look like? How should the controls operate? How well is the music synchronised to events within the game? The ability to grasp and manage complex interdependent tasks quickly is vital in this role.

Entry, training and career development

There is no clear, defined entry point for games testers within many games studios. Some studios rotate roles within the team, so it is often likely that games programmers working on one project will also be testers for another project. If you have strong PC skills then it is likely that you will be able to change roles within games development projects in order to achieve your career goals.

Localisation tester

Key tasks and skills

Before games written for the UK market can be sold in other countries, they may require changes to be made to the screen displays or the instruction manuals. It is the role of the localisation tester to test such games during their transition from the original English into the localised version that will be used in the country of purchase. The localisation tester will ensure all translations made are correct and proof-read all the manuals.

Entry, training and career development

Fluency in foreign languages (mainly European) is essential, as is a good understanding of the English language. A good understanding of PCs is important – and you must enjoy playing computer games!

Working within the computer games industry

A career in the computer games industry will involve working in a highly competitive market with many commercial pressures (just think of the Christmas games sales every year). With so many excellent games companies operating within the sector, often the only difference between success and failure is how quickly they can get their game into the shops. Whilst working in the computer games industry can be fun (yes, you _do_ get to play all the games and include a few 'secret' passwords and tricks that only the development team know about), it is hard work. Computer games design, in particular, requires a lot more skill than most games programmers are willing to admit.

More often than not, you will be working in a team throughout the lifecycle of the product, from designing the game to completing the finished version ready for sale. During the early stages of development, the average team size is small (around six people), but towards the end of the project, when pressure to get the game completed and marketed is greater, the team will reach nearer 30 in number. Throughout the project you will often need to communicate with non-IT people, such as artists and sound engineers, so communication and planning skills will be important. These skills are taught on degree courses, which is another reason why there is a demand for high-calibre graduates in this industry.

Salary

Despite the excitement and kudos often associated with a career in the much-hyped computer games industry, most games designers, developers and testers tend to be slightly lower paid than similar positions in the commercial programming sector. The average entry level salary is around £15,000–£19,000 for a games developer, rising to over £40,000. In addition, you can expect to earn royalties based on sales. Specific information on particular game companies and development studios can usually be found on their own Web sites (again, have a look in _The Edge_ for company information).

125

Chris *is a Games Programmer.*

I graduated from university with a 2:1 degree in Software Engineering, and joined a commercial software house, writing programs in C and C++. Whilst I enjoyed my work, after a while, I found that it became a bit repetitive. I suppose all programming does after a while, but I am a bit impatient and felt I needed a more dynamic working environment. Luckily my programming skills allowed me to move fairly easily to a games development company in London. I really enjoy the work here, it's completely different to commercial programming, but the importance is still as great. Our deadlines are very strict indeed, which often means many long days, but it's very satisfying work. And, just in case you were wondering, no, I don't spend all day playing games (that's someone else's job)!

9 *Careers outside development and support*

Computer sales

In some ways, being in computer sales is one of the most important roles within the IT profession, and it is probably one of the best paid too. Computer sales staff provide business selling the computer hardware, software and services needed to solve problems and increase profitability. Whilst sales staff have an understanding of computer systems, they will often rely on IT specialists to help them during the sales process, both before and after the sale (*pre-sales support* and *post-sales support*). A good knowledge of business, often in a specific field such as retail or personnel systems, is essential, as is a shrewd mind for figures. Whilst salaries for sales staff are usually high, part of their salary is usually in the form of a commission, based on the value of the sale. Many top sales staff are graduates, who can combine their technical expertise with management skills they have developed. However, there are opportunities for existing professionals from many diverse backgrounds to move into IT sales, maybe after performing a marketing or pre-sales support role first.

Salary

Salaries in sales can vary enormously depending on the amount of commission received. An average salary (excluding commission) could be anywhere between £30,000–£50,000, but six-figure salaries are achievable in many of the larger IT companies.

Angela *works in the sales department for a major systems software company.*

Although I'm in sales, my official job title is Account Manager – it's a bit more customer friendly than salesman (or saleswoman)! Working for a large software house whose products are written for IBM mainframe computers, I don't really need to 'sell' products as such – technical support managers tend to come to me first with their problems! In my business I deal with the customer all the time, either the technical support manager, or sometimes the IT director. Whatever, they will have a clear picture of what they need from me, although they might not know of our latest piece of software that might help them. This is why I tend to bring a few technical specialists with me after the initial meeting, so they can demonstrate the product and answer any specific queries that the customer may have (apart from 'how much does it cost?' – that's my job). I do understand the products from a technical point of view as I started off as a computer programmer and then spent a few years as a team leader in a technical support environment before I eventually moved into sales.

The job is very demanding; I have to travel a lot and meet customers at their convenience, not mine – so if that means meeting them at 7pm on a Friday, then that's when I've got to go. Luckily, I enjoy meeting people and having a good chat about their specific requirements and what they've been up to recently – it all helps build rapport with the customer. The only downside is that the business lunches tend to play havoc with my figure! If I could sum up my role in one sentence, I would say 'hard work, but full of perks!'.

Technical author

It is the job of the technical author to design and produce technical publications and documents that will be required by people using computer systems. You might think that this task would be performed by the technical support and development staff – in some smaller companies this is probably true, but in larger companies, there is usually a person with technical writing skills to perform this task. A typical situation a technical author might encounter is being asked to write documentation such as:

▌ user guides (for people new to the computer application);
▌ technical reference manuals (for technicians who must support the computer systems);
▌ technical magazines, flysheets and any other form of written communication.

A technical author needs a rare set of skills, combining the roles of author and publisher with those of an IT specialist. Whilst word-processing packages are widely used within the IT industry, a technical author will often use more sophisticated document-composition software, similar to the packages used within the electronic publishing industry.

Salary

Starting salaries tend to fall in the range £12,000–£15,000. Experienced technical authors can expect £30,000–£40,000.

IT trainer

With the phenomenal growth in the use of IT, the role of the trainer is becoming ever more important. Training can cover all areas of IT, such as hardware, software and networking compo-nents, but also many non-technical areas, such as report writing, project management and presentation skills. The scope of the training itself can vary from course to course, and can range from teaching a small group of people a few simple instructions on a PC to providing classroom-based training for a whole department on the use of a new software product.

The most important skill required for an IT trainer is to be able to communicate effectively. Basically, you must be _understood_. Obviously, you should possess good technical skills, usually in one or two main areas, but general IT skills would be helpful as well.

It is worth remembering that you will often be presenting new material to the class for most of the time during a normal day, either explaining the subject to them or helping them solve any problems they might be experiencing. You will need to remain calm, patient and, above all, professional at all times. Not an easy job, especially when your authority might be challenged by some of the smarter students in your class! Most of the top consultancy companies and IT vendors have a training division, so this would be a good place to start.

Salary

Graduate IT trainers working for an IT consultancy company can expect to earn between £18,000 and £20,000. Freelance IT trainers working for a large IT vendor can expect to earn around £2,000 a week.

Further information

Lots of information on training companies, courses, qualifications and jobs can be found in specialist magazines aimed at training professionals, such as *IT Trainer*.

Katherine *is a freelance IT trainer.*

On graduating from Hull University, I became a UNIX systems programmer, as I had picked up a lot of UNIX knowledge during my course. However, I soon realised that I preferred helping people understand the UNIX operating system than I did programming and supporting it! I suspect this was partly due to the fact that I like meeting people and I consider myself to be a good communicator, especially on technical issues.

For the next few years I worked in the training department of a computer vendor and enjoyed myself immensely. Not only did I have to provide a technical role in planning the course structure and content, but I also had to manage the external contractors we employed for specific courses.

Recognising the increasing demand for IT trainers, I then became a freelance contractor, giving me the freedom to train people in many other companies. Working in the M4 corridor, I am now employed by a number of major computer vendors who use freelance contractors, such as Hewlett-Packard and Sun Microsystems. The work is varied, and I do get a lot of free time between courses, which is quite nice in the demanding world of IT. If I had a dislike in being a trainer, it would be the amount of travelling I can sometimes end up doing between customer sites – still, as a contractor, my salary more than makes up for that!

10 Careers in e-commerce

Unless you have been living on another planet for the last few years, you will not have escaped the publicity surrounding electronic commerce (e-commerce). Just about every daily newspaper has featured regular articles discussing the significance of the Internet and e-commerce. The subject is even more vigorously covered in business newspapers, such as the *Financial Times*. E-commerce affects everyone, not just the IT profession, and it is already being accepted by the consumer society. In an attempt to discover how aware everyday people were of e-commerce, a recent survey discovered that Lastminute.com was the second most recognised Internet business Web site, behind Amazon.com (the virtual bookshop).

E-commerce is nothing more than the buying and selling of products and services by businesses and consumers over the Internet. To be fair, the concept of e-commerce has been around for years, but was not commercially viable until recently, when the capability to send payment (credit card) details over the Internet securely became possible.

The UK government has not been slow to recognise the importance of e-commerce either. New measures have now come into operation that are designed to help encourage new e-businesses: 100 per cent of IT equipment investment costs (hardware, software and online infrastructure costs) can now be written off against tax as can a proportion of research and development costs.

The phenomenal growth of e-commerce throughout the UK and the rest of the world is a double-edged sword. E-commerce offers a great number of exciting new opportunities for business and IT professionals alike. Unfortunately, with the current shortage in Internet skills, many businesses will miss out on the massive boom that is sweeping the country.

Types of e-commerce companies

Despite the fact that these companies appear to operate in a similar way, most business analysts now suggest there are three distinct types of e-commerce company. Whilst this may seem an unnecessary classification to the average person, if you are aiming for a top job in e-commerce, you should make it a priority to find out as much as you can about the industry. Don't forget, whilst there have been many successful business start-ups on the Internet, attracting top graduates with share options and high salaries, there have been even more disasters. Unfortunately, many top graduates (and not just IT graduates) have been lured away from good jobs in successful 'high-street' organisations to join these new exciting Internet start-up companies, only to find themselves unemployed a few months later when the company declares itself bankrupt. Don't forget, an Internet company is, in many ways, just the same as a traditional company – if the underlying business idea is poor, then it stands little chance of success.

The start-up company

Start-ups are the companies who have received most of the publicity to date – the true 'dot com' companies. These companies, such as Lastminute.com, Amazon.com, eBay and America Online have no real 'bricks and mortar' infrastructure – they are true 'cyber-entities'. These companies have been successful (and therefore offer attractive salaries and perks to attract and retain staff) because they have taken traditional business methods and completely transformed them. One of the best known examples of this is the Internet bookshop, Amazon.com. This company, offering high levels of personalisation, matched with an enormous range of titles, offers a service that a traditional bookshop on the high street could never match.

The spin-off company

The spin-off company is one where an e-commerce business operation has been developed on the back of an existing traditional business operation. Recently, there have been some notable examples of spin-off companies: Egg, hived off from the Prudential, and Smile, a spin-off from the Cooperative Bank. Being a spin-off company means the existing 'bricks and mortar' company still exists as a separate operation, but is supplemented by its Internet offspring. Spin-off companies are driven by their desire to attract new 'Internet-aware' customers quickly without alienating their existing customers. Setting up a spin-off company is one successful way that the company's directors can state their intentions to eventually move all of the business online.

Probably the best known example of a spin-off e-commerce company is Freeserve, the Internet service provider (ISP), which was spun-off from Dixons, the electrical retailer. Not only did Freeserve revolutionalise the way people accessed the Internet (by making it free), forcing established ISPs to quickly drop their prices, they also managed a successful stock market flotation as well, just nine months after start-up.

Company profile: Freeserve

Business plan: *To provide free Internet access to everyday PC users.*

Up to 1998, John Pluthero, a 36-year-old former grammar school boy from Colchester, was working in Dixon's distribution and aftersales department – hardly what you might call a classic IT role. Even as a relative stranger to the high-tech world of IT, he convinced the chairman of Dixon's, Sir Stanley Kalms, of his idea for Freeserve – providing free access to millions of Web sites for anyone with a PC. All they had to do was to walk into any Dixon's store and collect a CD containing all the Internet access software. At a time when demand for the Internet was soaring throughout the UK, but with the costs of the telephone call being prohibitive, it was nothing short of revolutionary.

Approach and planning
John was sensible in realising he did not possess the technical skills to plan his Web site and drafted in an expert to help him. Peter Wilkinson (also now a millionaire), then part-

owner of the Web site design firm Planet Online, sketched out the draft design for Freeserve on the back of a napkin on a train journey from Yorkshire. The rest, as they say, is history.

Business success
Freeserve, despite strong competition, is the UK's largest ISP, attracting over 1.3 million users. Like many ISPs, its profits derive from charging advertisers to sell their products.

The 'bricks and clicks' company

The 'bricks and clicks' company (or 'clicks and mortar') as the name suggests, is a traditional organisation that sees the Internet as a new marketing tool – a way to increase existing sales or produce new sources of revenue. High street retailers such as The Gap or Tesco are good examples of this type of company – the e-commerce business is just an extension of an existing brand, not a completely new one, as with Egg or Smile.

Types of e-commerce transactions

Typically there are three types of e-commerce within which all categories of business transaction will take place:

- business to business e-commerce;
- business to consumer e-commerce;
- consumer to consumer e-commerce.

Business to business e-commerce

Business to business (B2B) e-commerce allows two businesses to trade with each other directly over the Internet. It is a major transformation from the way traditional business has operated, removing the need for huge supply chains and 'middle-men'. In the world of IT this is best exemplified by businesses now dealing

135

directly with IT hardware and software manufacturers (such as Cisco and IBM), via their Web sites and ordering products online.

Of course, the B2B market is still very much in the embryonic stages of growth, but the prospects for enormous future growth are good. Figure 10.1 shows the estimated value of B2B transactions against all commercial transactions. In 1999 B2B e-commerce accounted for a mere $215 million – by 2004 e-commerce could be worth $5.7 trillion.

Business to consumer e-commerce

This is probably the most popular form of e-commerce, being essentially 'electronic retailers' or, in Internet jargon, 'e-tailers'. The concept is fairly straightforward: think of a good retail idea; build a Web site; start selling directly over the Internet. Obviously in business, nothing is quite as simple as this, but I'm sure you can appreciate the idea. There are of course risks: not everything sells better over the Internet – you might not, for instance, want to buy fruit or vegetables over the Internet (how would you select a nice ripe pear or an over-ripe tomato?). Table 10.1 lists the most popular product categories selected by consumers on the Web.

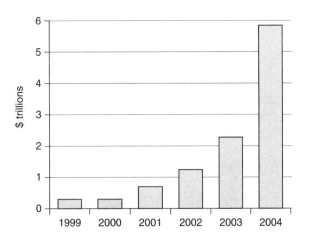

Figure 10.1   Estimated value of B2B transactions against all commercial transactions

Table 10.1   The most popular product categories selected during e-commerce transactions

Rank	Product
1	computer products (hardware, software)
2	books
3	music (CDs, videos)
4	financial services
5	entertainment
6	home electronics
7	clothing
8	gifts and flowers
9	travel services
10	toys
11	tickets
12	information

Personal profile

Mirella Barnes has been in the lingerie trade for more than 15 years; the only business decision she made behind her husband's back was to buy a PC and connect to the Internet. Now her Web site, www.lingerieuk.co.uk, counts for one-third of her turnover. 'What I like most,' she says, 'is by the time I open my shop door in the morning, I have already done about £500 pounds worth of business.' Mirella recently became Business Woman of the Year in Nottingham and is planning even greater things with her Web site. Mirella has been successful because she has used IT to make a successful business better – her core business activities have not changed. Her Web site is popular as it helps women who find it difficult to get the right size in the shops, but it's also useful for men too. One man who works on an oil rig in the North Sea once used the site to order lingerie for his wife on her birthday instead of flowers. He reported back to Mirella that it went down so well, he's now a regular customer!

Consumer to consumer e-commerce

This category of e-commerce is probably the most risky as the consumer is both the supplier and buyer of products – an auction in other words. Recent trends show a gradual migration away from this type of e-commerce towards the much more lucrative B2B e-commerce.

Company profile: QXL

Business plan: *To develop a UK competitor to US online auction sites such as eBay and Onsale.*

Tim Jackson was a journalist working for the *Financial Times* when he decided to change his career direction and enter the world of e-commerce. Being impressed by the early success of US auction sites, such as eBay and Onsale, he decided to set up his own UK-based auction site. Quixell launched in 1997, selling various items purchased from manufacturers and distributors, but in 1998 changed its name to QXL and began offering person-to-person auctions.

Approach and planning
The key drivers behind setting up the site were very clear for Tim Jackson. He was already well aware of the benefits the Internet could bring to business: 24-hour ordering; no need to leave your home or office; the ability to offer consumers thousands of products at the click of a button – and then have them delivered to your front door.

Business success
QXL now sells more than 871,000 items to more than 246,000 customers in five European countries. So successful is it that a leading market analyst organisation voted QXL the number one e-commerce site in the UK in September 1999. With sites now open in Germany, France, Italy and Norway, the future is looking good for QXL.

Key recruiters

──────── Company profile: IBM ────────

Revenue: $29 billion
Profit: $7billion
Employees: 136,000 (worldwide)

E-commerce strategy

IBM is already the world's largest supplier of outsourcing and services and hopes to maintain that position by providing IT services to support e-commerce. IBM's consulting arm, Global Services, is now split into several divisions to reflect the changing focus of IT consulting:

- E-commerce Services covers IT relating to the retail sector, such as secure payment systems, privacy protection and online transaction processing.
- Enablement Services provides businesses with messaging systems to allow them to work directly with other online businesses. IBM's Hosted Business Application Services links Web-based systems to core business applications.
- E-business Accelerator offers online consulting and an assessment of a company's readiness to move towards e-commerce.

Typical clients: Cable and Wireless Communications, Arcadia Group, Ford Motors.

──────── Company profile: EDS ────────

Revenue: $16.9 billion
Profit: $1.1 billion
Employees: 20,000

E-commerce strategy

EDS still holds the number one position in UK consulting and hopes to hold onto it with the launch of its E-Solutions Unit, a consulting division specialising in e-commerce solutions and services. The unit is organised around the company's four key business areas: management consulting; solutions consulting; business process management and information solutions and offers strategic planning and implementation of e-commerce solutions.

Typical clients: US Department of Defense, Inland Revenue.

Company profile: ICL

Revenue: £3,343.7 million
Profit: £117.6 million loss (or £40.9 million before exceptional factors)
Employees: 3,000+ in consulting, 800 in e-commerce

E-commerce strategy
ICL's e-commerce services are run from Helsinki and in 1998 created revenues of £80 million. ICL specialises in creative Internet technology and has developed technology for WAP applications, first-stop Web sites (or portals) and interactive shopping. ICL has a global alliance with Microsoft although it does work with 900 other non-Microsoft products.

Typical clients: BBC, Freeserve, Sega Dreamcast, Electrolux.

Top jobs in e-commerce

The concept of the Web as a trading and communication medium is now firmly established within society as a whole. With 9 million people online in the UK, a figure that is expected to rocket to 23 million by the end of 2001, and five new Internet sites going live every week, opportunities exist to join or work for companies who are leading the way in e-commerce.

Judy Gibbons _is UK Director, MSN._

Judy Gibbons left college with an honours degree in civil engineering, with little thought of moving into IT, let alone ending up with a top job in IT. In fact, out of all the modules she studied as part of her degree course, she found the computing module the least appealing. When she graduated from Brighton Polytechnic (now Brighton University) in 1977 she went, as planned, into the construction industry.

Despite working on large construction projects in the Middle East, an opportunity that many others would have longed for, she soon realised that she needed a career change. After considering alternative careers in advertising and law, she decided to move into IT, and found a job with Hewlett Packard, an IT hardware and software manufacturer, as a graduate trainee. It wasn't long though before Judy ended up in California's Silicon Valley, but while enjoying living in the US, in the long-term she knew it was not for her. Her next move was to Apple, makers of the successful Macintosh computer, and it was here she had her first experience of multimedia computing – using computers with other media such as telecommunications. From that early work, pioneered by Apple, the interactive CD ROM industries and the video games industry have now developed.

Judy now leads a team of producers, editors, designers, software engineers and sales and marketing professionals – over 50 in total who look after Microsoft's consumer Internet business in the UK. Judy is convinced the Internet will generate a huge amount of business growth in the UK; after all, she's well aware of the amount of talent there is there.

Microsoft is a leading supplier of Internet technology and is always looking for highly-motivated individuals who can work well in a team. At Microsoft, according to Judy, about 70 per cent of a person's career development is on the job – based on challenging work assignments. The rest is based on a personal development plan, which is driven by the individual and agreed by a manager. Judy is on the record as saying (not surprisingly!) that she thinks Microsoft is a great company to work for and would readily recommend the computer industry to anyone seeking a rewarding and satisfying career. MSN can be contacted at:

5th Floor
189 Shaftesbury Avenue
London
WC2H 8JB
or by telephone on: (0870) 601 0100

Company profile: Liv4now.com

Liv4now.com is a mixture between a community site, providing the opportunity for chatting to like-minded people on the topical subjects of the day (fashion, sport, food, cars, clubs and so on), and a serious 'help' site, where you can visit to buy theatre tickets, book a holiday or obtain career advice.

Personal profile

Serena Doshi, Managing Director and Co-Founder

Serena Doshi co-founded Liv4now.com in March 1999 and has acted as Managing Director ever since. Serena had over six years of media experience prior to joining the Internet revolution. She spent four years at Arthur Andersen where she worked with companies such as BSkyB, ITN, Virgin Radio and WPP and left Arthur Andersen in 1997 to join the investment bank Schroders, now part of Citigroup, where she worked on mergers and acquisitions in their Media Division.

——— *Personal profile* ———

Ewan MacLeod, Chief Technical Officer and Co-Founder

Ewan MacLeod co-founded Liv4now.com in March 1999 after a chance meeting with Serena Doshi in November 1998, when he called round to fix her broken printer. At Liv4now.com, Ewan is currently responsible for all technology operations and is in charge of Community Management on the site. Liv4now.com is not Ewan's first taste of Internet life. In 1996 Ewan founded and managed The Outer Edge, a community site for teenagers at AOL before working with Virgin.net in establishing an online community site for teenagers. Ewan holds a BSc degree in Information Management.

——— *Personal profile* ———

Paul Rogers, Editor

Paul Rogers joined the Liv4now.com team in October 1999 and is responsible for the editorial content on the site. Before joining Liv4now.com, Paul worked as Sub-Editor and writer on *GQ* magazine, where he interviewed Sophie Dahl, Nick Moran and Debbie Harry, amongst others. Prior to joining *GQ*, Paul worked as an international sports writer for *Total Sport* as a football journalist, and a freelance music journalist for *The Independent*, *Sky* and a few other publications. Like many founders of Internet companies, he originally had no interest in the Internet, claiming '… the Internet was for geeks. I didn't even see the point of e-mail.'

Further information

Information Society Initiative

The Information Society Initiative (ISI) is a partnership between industry and government to help British business thrive in the information society. A network of around 100 ISI Local Support Centres operates in the UK in partnership with the Business Link network in England and their equivalents in Wales, Scotland and Northern Ireland.

The Local Support Centres can help you successfully exploit IT by providing the following services:

- impartial and expert advice;
- consultancy and IT audits;
- training;
- access to IT equipment;
- discussion with other business people;
- Internet services.

Contact information

Free booklets and lots of other information can be obtained by:

calling the ISI Business Infoline on (0845) 715 2000;
e-mailing ISI on info@isi.gov.uk;
visiting the ISI Web site at www.isi.gov.uk.

11

How to become an Internet millionaire

If you have been a regular reader of the business and financial papers over the last year or so, you will no doubt have read about the incredible number of Internet millionaires that have cropped up from nowhere – the 'dot.com millionaires'. During the latter part of 1999 and into the early parts of 2000, it did appear that anyone wanting to become an Internet millionaire should register a company with a '.com' suffix and wait for the money to pour in. It was a plan that for a while did work; the Internet was seen as crucial for survival; anyone who wasn't online would not be able to compete and fall by the wayside. Eager investors wanting to make a quick profit ensured the demand for Internet start-ups was kept artificially high, along with their share price.

It was only a matter of time before the stock market caught up with the Internet boom, adjusting share prices to match the *real* value of many of the new Internet start-ups. Millions were wiped off their value in a matter of weeks. Of late, however, there has been a return to normality and stability within the IT sector, but the perceived long-term viability of many dot.coms still remains an issue. Don't be fooled though. No one is suggesting the Internet has become redundant, but the institutions that finance such ventures are now much more selective and cautious about investing in companies that have very few (if any) assets and take years to return a profit. As always, lessons can be learnt, and it is often precisely this that differentiates the foolish amateurs from the successful professionals. Learning the lessons from previous Internet start-ups will not guarantee that you will become the next Internet millionaire, but it will hopefully ensure that you won't be the next Internet failure. Whether your aim is to go free-lance, try out a new business as a 'hobby' or if you really think you have a multi-million pound idea, the following 10-point plan should help.

The top 10 rules for starting your own e-business

1. Research your idea

Great business ventures start from simple ideas. Most ideas usually start with the question: 'what can I sell over the Internet?' Simple really – clothes, books, CDs, fruit and vegetables (a bit messy possibly?), cars and toys and advice.

2. Think of a business name

Unlike the high street, where established brands have market share, people are attracted to trade on the Internet (which could be *your* Web site) for all sorts of reasons. If you get customers to buy into your brainwave, they just might be tempted to spare a few seconds on your site if it has a catchy name. The wackier the name, the better chance you may have of someone typing it in. If you really are stuck, try and find out what's cool language and what isn't – a trip to the local cinema at matinee time is worth a try. Be inspired by a US company that saw its stock rise by over 200 per cent after it renamed itself Fatbrain.com.

However, in the current climate, which has seen many dot.coms go bust, there is a case for companies to select a traditional or established trading name. Until the trading situation improves, stability is the name of the game.

3. Register your domain name as soon as possible

If you want to trade as a company over the Internet, you will need a domain name, such as myshop.co.uk. You can use any normal word, but you'll have to be quick as all the sensible, meaningful names will have probably gone. Of course, if you do manage to get hold of a really good domain name, you could nearly become a millionaire overnight by selling it onto a major organisation. There are numerous companies offering domain names for rent or for sale, which can be found on most general Internet Web sites and portals. In the UK, you could use a company called www.domainnames.co.uk. They charge £125 + VAT plus a fee of £50 every two years after that. Alternatively, try www.easily.co.uk, www.portland.co.uk or www.netlink.co.uk.

4. Advertise your site

A Web site that no one knows about is worthless. To help people find it you will need to register it on some of the big search engines, such as AltaVista, Excite and Yahoo!. Look out for the 'Add a site' button on their Web sites. You may need to reregister your site a few months later if you slip down the rankings table as new sites are added. For guaranteed results you can pay a company such as http://1st-place-Web-site-promotion.co.uk to ensure your site comes near the top of the search results. This will cost around £500 to set it up plus £1,000 a year. Not cheap, but presence in the marketplace should bring its own rewards.

5. Make sure you have the right skills

Whilst any form of IT investment might expect the candidate director to have some knowledge of the technologies the business will use, it is not a requirement for budding Internet millionaires. One director of an Internet company listed on the Alternative Investment Market (AIM) once stated that 'we have no experience of the Internet. We have cross-border transaction skills.' The share price doubled in a day. There are enough consultancies around now who will provide you with all the technology you need, build your Web site and support your business operation. If you do employ someone to help set up your site, make sure you can update it yourself later. Choose a popular program such as Macromedia Dreamweaver or Adobe GoLive and include a photo editor such as Photoshop/Imageready or Fireworks.

6. Make sure you are ready for the challenge

The Internet is a wild, uncontrolled jungle where only the daring will survive. A nice new pin-striped suit will not protect you from disaster. Do you have the right frame of mind to see this through? If you have youth on your side you are halfway there – mid-thirties seems to be the unofficial 'upper limit' for anyone wanting to be taken seriously. Oh, and by the way, ties are a no-no.

7. Identify potential sources of funding

If you walk into your local bank and ask your bank manager for a six-figure loan or overdraft facility to launch (yet another) Internet company, he will think you are mad and show you the door. A more sensible choice, and one which has proved successful to many Internet millionaires in the fledging days of their start-ups, is to approach one the many venture capital companies (known to many e-millionaires as VCs) who will provide start-up capital in return for a stake in your business.

8. Ensure you have a watertight business plan

A director of a leading venture capital outfit has identified five key factors that VCs look out for: the team, the concept, the business plan, the competition and the financial projections. You may have noticed that these factors are nothing new to the world of business – in fact they are the very cornerstones of successful businesses all over the world. E-business, in this sense, is no different and should not be thought of as anything else. The last item is often the most hard to determine, as many Internet companies trade for many years without actually making a profit – the investment is usually in the profit *potential*. That's a big gamble for many VCs, as many start-up Internet companies don't have any sales either. Still, it didn't prevent Apax Partners and other leading VCs investing between £5 million and £20 million for a 25 per cent stake in Internet start-ups. With this amount of investment, few VCs would be happy to allow the Internet start-up company to be run by a spotty student in an old parka – they will almost always insist on bringing in their own management team to keep the company in order.

9. Establish your e-credibility

To the casual observer of IT terminology, networking is something to do with cables and computers. To the potential Internet millionaire, networking is an essential 'soft' skill involving building a rapport with like-minded people and, in doing so, developing a list of useful contacts in the Internet world. Being on first name terms with some of the larger VCs is an admirable position to be in. Look at www. digitalpeople.org – it's a contact group involving venture capitalists.

10. Float on the stock market

This is where the fun really starts. Floating your company on the stock market through an Initial Public Offering (IPO) will hopefully make you a paper millionaire overnight, as a result of stock options you hold. You will need to involve the services of various legal and financial bodies, but as many investment institutions are happy to be paid in share options, you might get away without paying them in cash. If you are really lucky, you will not have to hold on to your shares for too long before you can cash them in and realise your first million!

Joining a dot.com

Not so long ago, top IT staff sat in meetings dreaming of winning the lottery or maybe even writing a bestseller and then retiring to some idyllic country retreat. Today's pipe dream is totally different: stock options in a dot.com, an IPO on the stock market and a small island in the Caribbean.

According to the the *Sunday Times* Rich List, the Internet is the fastest growing source of wealth in the UK. In the UK alone, over 50 Internet companies are expected to go public this year. With the ongoing consolidation and maturity of European networks and mobile technologies, many top industry analysts and e-commerce directors are expecting Europe to take the lead in e-commerce.

The problem with making a million from stock options in a dot.com is the fact that your investment (and nest egg) is entirely dependent on the performance of the stock you possess. If you had to stay with a dot.com for three years before you could sell your shares, you would be extremely naïve to count on your paper millions.

With careful planning though, there is no reason why you can't become the next Internet millionaire and follow in the footsteps of Mike Lynch, the Cambridge-based graduate whose stake in Internet software vendor Autonomy made him the UK's first Internet half-billionaire (he's worth £500 million). On a more conservative (but equally impressive) scale, Jason New, 25, works with Internet specialist Broadvision, building e-commerce services for clients such as Vodafone. Not only does he enjoy a £50,000 salary, he also holds £1 million in stock options, which he is able to sell for £20,000 a month. Jason plans to retire at 40.

As a top graduate (or a high-flier with a large employer, such as an IT consultancy), you will be a prime target for a dot.com. This could be the start of a lucrative and rewarding career; you should expect to receive some healthy stock options and joining bonuses, but you could equally get your fingers burnt on the way up the ladder. The Internet recruitment specialists Venture Partnership offer this advice to people who have been approached by a dot.com:

▌ First of all, ask some basic questions about money (their money), such as whether or not they are being funded and by whom. If your prospective employer is being funded by one of the leading venture capitalists, you could assume they have shown due diligence on their business plan. Names such as Atlas Venture, Arts Alliance, New Media Investors and Global Retail Partners are really active in the industry and well respected.

▌ Look at the management team. What experience do they have of the market they are in? Many companies fail, not because of the business plan, but because the people running the company have no track record in that specific market. The safe bet is to go for older, serial entrepreneurs with a good track record. The stock market also likes these types of people – they have done it once before, they can do it again.

▌ Assess their business plan. Is there really a sustainable market for the product or service the company is offering? What competition do they have and what competitive edge do they have over them? Despite the bad press that has sometimes been aimed at companies such as Freeserve and Lastminute.com, they have always had good business plans and a clear direction for the company. Look at the company's expansion plans. In a global market, market share is vital for survival.

Going it alone

If you are an MBA graduate from a leading business school or a born entrepreneur, then you will probably enter the world of IT and the Internet under your own steam; you will either be head-hunted by an existing Internet company or you will start your own IT business using your skills and business contacts. If you fit into one of these two categories, this book is not for you.

If you *do* think you have an idea that can be transformed (with a bit of help) into a successful and viable business venture over the Internet, then great – go for it. There is no reason why you cannot become the next dot.com millionaire (on paper at least) – the opportunities are out there; the biggest problem is staying in business.

Too many Internet start-ups (including some big names, such as Boo.com) were forced out of business prematurely for all sorts of reasons. Make sure you keep your head above water and your eyes on your business accounts! The harsh truth is painfully simple; most venture capitalists estimate that no more than 5 per cent of Internet start-ups receive the funding they seek. In fact, directors at Durlacher, one of the leading venture capitalist companies, readily admit they don't have enough hours in the day to read most of the business plans they receive, let alone assess them for funding.

Whilst there are many people who have made millions overnight from floating their 'dot.com' companies on the Stock Exchange, there are hundreds more business people who are quietly starting their own e-businesses with only a small investment and a lot of business sense. Having your own Web site on the Internet allows you to market your business and sell your products online. Potential customers can then browse your site, e-mail you with enquiries, place electronic orders and pay for their goods with credit cards. The Web provides one of the best opportunities to start your own small business for a number of reasons:

- low operating costs (for *simple* operation, all you need is a PC, Internet access and a Web site);
- the ability to do business 24 hours a day, 365 days a year;
- the chance to reach a huge customer base and market your goods effectively.

Despite these exciting times, the world of IT is desperate for top graduates to employ and train as e-commerce specialists. Similarly, the world of business is keen to attract entrepreneurs who will develop their companies to meet the demands of operating in the information society. It's worth remembering that women can play an equal part in IT as well as men – women are now as keen to use the Internet as men are. Five years ago women made up just 10 per cent of the UK Internet community – now that figure has risen to 40 per cent. In a recent survey of Internet companies, over 30 per cent of them were registered and owned by women. The 27-year-old co-founder of Lastminute.com, Martha Lane Fox, has certainly helped balance the scales. Even though on paper she's a multi-millionairess, thanks to her share options in the company, she's not motivated by the money but simply excited by the prospect of her business growing faster and becoming even more successful. Not bad for someone who admits to 'knowing peanuts' about computers.

Building your own Web site

Trading on the Internet was once the sole province of large organisations who could rely on their IT, legal and accounts departments to ensure the transition went smoothly. Not any more. Today, many banks and specialist companies are falling over themselves to offer help in setting up an online shop. As well as providing help with setting up your Web-based 'shop-front', such organisations can also offer help with payment processing, Internet access, e-mail, small business advice and information, data storage, accounting and banking. Some will even sell or allow you to lease a computer.

Of course, you may not need any of these services – some of the early successes were based purely on creating a Web site to determine the level of interest in the overall concept. Trading was not seen as important as advertising and getting the site well known amongst potential customers. If you want to start with something less flashy than some of the products being offered there is a wide range of options available to you.

For instance, the Microsoft Office 2000 suite includes a program for helping you design and build Web pages. Alternatively, you can buy packages like Microsoft's *Front Page* or *Dreamweaver* relatively cheaply or even download Web page design programs from the Internet. CD ROM Internet connection software, available free from magazines, such as Netscape's *Communicator* and Microsoft's *Internet Explorer*, also provide many useful Web design and security configuration programs. Web design is simple in theory, and most people should be able to create a decent Web site using HTML in a weekend. They may not be the whizziest or the most striking on the Internet, but they will be respectable efforts. Web site design is not rocket science, but like any new skill, following a few simple rules will make all the difference. There is, of course, lots of information on Web site design available both on the Internet and in bookshops and libraries.

In addition, Internet Service Providers, such as Freeserve, BT and Virgin, are more than willing to host your Web site for business use. Many will even provide design software free or at very low rates.

Top tips for building a Web site

- Keep it simple – you are not trying to win the Turner prize for art.
- Stick to a few basic colours and shapes.
- Keep the number of 'clicks' required to navigate around your Web site to a minimum – people will soon lose interest if they haven't found the Web page they're looking for quickly.
- Provide an e-mail address as a contact point for information and assistance.
- Keep it accurate and up-to-date.
- Moving images look great, but too many are a distraction.

Using commercial packages

There are many commercial packages available on the market and it is important that you first decide what your requirements are before deciding which one to buy. Some of the more basic packages offer simple online shops free, others charge fees depending on how large an operation you require. For example, a simple online shop offering up to 10 different products will cost much less than a shop allowing you space for hundreds of products.

The National Westminster Bank's *BusinessEdge* package allows you to build a basic Web site for up to 100 products with card payment facilities. Costs are £45 a month or you can have the site built for between £50 and £100. It also offers free online banking, marketing and accountancy packages, a data backup service (£17 a month), Internet Service Provider and e-mail services and business advice. You can also buy Internet-ready PCs from the bank too (just in case you forget, I presume).

Barclays' *Clearlybusiness* allows Freeserve users to set up a basic Webshop from about £55 a month, plus an annual fee of £125 to Worldpay for its card payment facilities. Bigger shops will cost a bit more. In addition you can also build your own Web site (with support) and buy a domain name. Barclays also supplies three-year deals on leasing computers connected to an ISP and an e-business guide from about £30 a month.

Top tips for using Internet trading packages

▍ Plan your operation well. Forget the technology. Concentrate on the business requirements.
▍ Do not buy more than you need.
▍ Determine the pay-back period for any package you buy. How long will it take to pay for itself?
▍ Try before you buy. If possible, set up a trial on the company's Web site

Getting finance

Unfortunately, we can't all rely on rich friends and family to fund our Internet start-ups. Don't worry, there are a number of investment companies who will show an interest in your idea if it has potential. Reading the articles in quality newspapers, you may think the only way of raising finance is through the major city investment banks – well, that's one way and good luck to you. An alternative approach (and one that is becoming increasingly popular) is to use organisations such as First Tuesday. This is a UK organisation that links venture capitalists with Internet entrepreneurs. If the membership statistics of this 'Internet club' are anything to go by, then you should expect to see a few more Internet millionaires being created before the end of the year – in the last five months membership has risen from just 1,000 to over 30,000. Looking at the stock market, the initial signs are promising. In the first half of 1999, venture capital firms pumped an incredible $5.7 billion into Internet companies, according to PriceWaterhouseCoopers. This year alone, Andersen Consulting will invest a further $1.2 billion in Internet start-ups.

The concept of a 'business angel' to help raise capital for Internet start-ups is now a firmly-established approach to funding. Rather than providing divine intervention (which may have helped prevent a few of the well-publicised Internet failures), the 'angels' in this case are usually entrepreneurs themselves who have already had a successful career in business. Business angels look for investment opportunities they can understand where they can see the key success factors for business – a good idea, a good product or service, a good team of people and a good understanding of the market and competition.

The National Business Angels Network (NBAN) specialises in bringing together firms looking for equity finance with private investors who are looking for investment opportunities. They have a wealth of experience, have many useful contacts and can help companies attract investment from business angels. Unfortunately, the angels they represent still get sent huge numbers of proposals that are too speculative in nature. In many cases, the business plan they are sent is incomplete or it is evident there has been little or no market research performed. In others, the business plan has not really been thought through or there is no awareness of what the competition is up to. NBAN's top tips for people seeking investment for dot.com companies or other Internet-related businesses include:

- Do your research – what are the competition doing and how well are they doing it?
- Make sure you have a critical mass of customers who are willing to trade online.
- Ensure your management team has good business skills or the potential to develop them.
- Offer a genuine branding opportunity – there is no such thing as customer loyalty on the Internet.

155

Peter Atalla *is Managing Director of student-net.*

Some of the recent Internet entrepreneurs who have become millionaires were lucky enough to have, as friends and family, an impressive list of merchant bankers, accountants, company directors and a fair amount of funding to help them on their way. Unfortunately, we are not all blessed with such fortune, so it is refreshing to discover that a bunch of students at Nottingham Trent University achieved similar success from their own efforts, having made many sacrifices along the way. What this case study proves is that if you have a good idea that you think (and more importantly, what potential investors think) is worth pursuing, you don't need friends in high places to help you.

The idea for student-net came one morning to Peter Atalla as he pondered the difficulty in finding a new flat for himself and his friends, only hours before he was due to sit a physics exam. His efforts to improve his situation eventually led him to what was to become the seed of his venture; a Web site that contained all the information necessary to help students survive and enjoy themselves at university. In true student style, he passed the idea around a few pals in the student union bar and after a few drinks he and his three pals decided to go for it. They formed student-net, basically a guide to student accommodation, college courses, bars, pubs and clubs whilst still struggling with their studies.

Apart from one, all the team were physics graduates whose ages ranged from 21 to 23. John Boardman was the only member who had studied computing, and with Peter Atalla had run a computer networking outfit at the university.

To get the venture off the ground they did almost risk everything, but managed to raise £55,000, putting them deep in debt. With the hours of unpaid work, other costs and expenses, their total investment in their Web site was probably nearer £300,000. For some time, they recall, the situation was really bad, with hardly any money left for food, which often meant going hungry. However, when they did eventually go online their site, www.student-net.co.uk, was being used by 20,000 people a week.

During 2000, Peter and his colleagues agreed a deal with US-based International Media Products Group and have sold the rights to student-net for £10 million. They will, however, remain as directors and the firm will remain in Nottingham. The company has now recruited the first 50 employees and more jobs are promised in the future.

Robin Stevens

In Robin's own words... 'this may sound crazy, but I didn't dream of making millions when I planned to launch my own Web site – I actually wanted to understand Java script and Visual Basic. My idea was to build an engine that could deal with more than three or four criteria and still deliver fast results. Ensuring a good response time, in my view anyway, is one of the fundamental building blocks of any decent Web site'.

Robin is, in fact, a 28-year-old IT contractor specialising in database design and administration, hardly the credentials of an Internet entrepreneur. The site cost him around £21,000, excluding development hours, which have been considerable. On top of an eight-hour day at work, Robin has often worked until 2 am developing his Web site. His site is nothing special, but it works; it allows potential house buyers to search for homes, specifying up to 100 criteria such as price, swimming pool, proximity to shops and roads and so on. It automatically e-mails or phones the vendor with the potential purchaser's details and also allows searches for local builders and solicitors. The service he provides is free initially, but when the site becomes more established, he hopes to charge a small fee per house, either paid by the estate agent or vendor. At this stage Robin does not want to bring in venture capitalists as he wants to remain in control of his venture.

Alex Lambert *is Creative Director of Surfworld.com*

Alex Lambert, 27, is another one of life's unlikely Internet millionaires, investing £100 to start a business that two years later was worth £1.1 million. His idea developed from his sporting obsession – surfing. From being a former junior international rower he became a surf 'dude', riding the waves near his home in North Devon by day and working in bars at night.

In terms of credentials, Alex would not stand out in the hi-tech world of IT, let alone the Internet; until two and a half years ago, he had never even used a computer. In a recent interview Alex admitted,'... the only surfing I knew anything about was on a board. I didn't have a clue about computers and had never touched the Web.'

It cost Alex £100 to set up his Web site, but he also received a £10,000 grant from the Prince's Trust. His Web site now receives up to 40,000 hits a month. During 2000 Alex sold the site to Names123.com, a subsidiary of the Internet group, Phase 8, making £1.1 million, but remains on as its creative director.

Further information

Web site and e-commerce software

Information on the National Westminster Bank's Internet package can be found on its Web site: www.natwest.com/businessedge

Information on Barclays' Clearlybusiness package can be found on its Web site: www.clearlybusiness.co.uk or www.business.barclays.net

Business Angels

For an information pack on the NBAN and how it can help you, contact the NBAN at:

National Business Angels Network
3rd Floor
40–42 Cannon Street
London
EC4N 6JJ
Tel: (020) 7329 2929
Information Pack Hotline: (020) 7329 4141
or via its Web site: www.nationalbusangels.co.uk

Business funding

The Prince's Trust can be contacted at:

Head Office
18 Park Square East
London
NW1 4LH
Tel: (020) 7543 1234 (Freephone (0800) 842842)
or via its Web site: www.princes-trust.org.uk

12 Getting in and getting on

Fast-track careers in IT

The current IT skills shortage shows no immediate signs of easing. As a consequence, many companies are now much more flexible towards graduate recruitment than they were five years ago. Whilst many IT companies now offer 'fast-track' graduate recruitment programmes for high-flying candidates, so desperate are some IT employers to recruit key skills, some are now offering fast-track recruitment programmes as well. For instance, PricewaterhouseCoopers, a leading UK IT consultancy, is trying to combat the skills shortage by offering successful applicants a job on the day of their interview. By using this fast-track approach, it hopes to recruit sufficient IT experts in key areas. Most in demand are systems integration and technical architecture consultants. Experience in Web technology such as Broadvision and ATG Dynamo is particularly valuable. According to a senior partner in the consultancy, over 70 per cent of their contracts are now based on e-business. A typical e-business project with the organisation involves between 10 and 15 software suppliers and requires consultants to integrate Web 'front-ends' with legacy systems (such as mainframe databases and order processing systems).

According to a director of one of the largest IT recruitment agencies, the big software houses are open-minded about admitting graduates from a variety of disciplines to their training programmes. However, for some projects, such as those relating to e-commerce, usually only IT graduates who have the technical skills to work directly on them succeed. Vance Kearney, the human resources vice-president of Oracle Corporation UK, has often stated that he would like to see more people without straight technical degrees coming out of university. The stereotype of the 'computer nerd' or 'geek' beavering away on some wacky technology is now firmly confined to the history books as far as IT is concerned.

Gaining the right skills

Unfortunately, there are many highly skilled graduates leaving university who wrongly assume that software companies are only interested in highly technical graduates. If you are one of them, get your CV polished up and get yourself registered with the top IT recruitment agencies right now. As Vance Kearney will tell you, Oracle are more interested in personal skills – people who are mature, outgoing, credible and able to learn. The company can always teach people the deeper knowledge of Oracle software that they will need, much more in fact than IT graduates will know.

According to James Flew, Director of Metzger Recruitment Consultants, which has been recruiting graduates for business for a number of years, a good degree is no longer enough for graduates aiming for a successful career. To be a fast-track candidate, you will need to use your degree as the bedrock on which you can build business and social skills. Candidates who can display flair, drive and business initiative as well as IT skills will ultimately succeed where others fail.

The ability for graduates to communicate both verbally and in writing is particularly important in an industry where the majority of users are not technically-minded. To achieve the highest levels of success in the IT industry you must be able to demonstrate clear communication skills at all levels, both with colleagues and clients.

Under a new scheme unveiled by London City University, IT departments are being encouraged to employ university IT students for four days a week as they complete their degrees. The university plans to offer up to 30 IT students a year the opportunity to combine paid work in an IT department with one day a week in lectures as part of an intensive four-year degree. After their first year at the university, students will be invited to join the programme, known as the Professional Pathway. Even though they will be gaining additional skills outside the university, they

161

will still attend the same lectures and complete the same coursework and exams as students on other IT courses within the university. To allow students to complete the Professional Pathway, the university will extend the course from 35 weeks to 45 weeks, making the overall duration of the course four years, only a year longer than conventional IT degrees.

The scheme has already attracted a number of software suppliers and banks, offering salaries ranging from £14,000 to £18,000 a year. A similar day-release scheme run by Salford University has also been well received by local employers, helping them reduce their recruitment costs considerably.

Graduate and postgraduate qualifications

You do not necessarily need a postgraduate degree, such as an MSc, PhD or MBA to succeed in the IT world. Drive and enthusiasm, more than anything, is what employers seek, but for a top job, reality dictates you will need at least a degree (preferably first class or upper-second) to start with. Fortunately, the IT industry has no rigid guidelines or expectations as to the type of degree required.

Some employers will insist on graduates possessing a degree in a strong IT subject such as Software Engineering, Computer Science or Computational Mathematics. Others will be happy to employ a graduate in any discipline. Bear in mind though, if you have a degree in a subject that contains only a limited amount of IT, for some employers it will be perfectly acceptable, for others you will be in direct competition with more technically qualified graduates. You need to do your research well and determine who are the most suitable companies to approach. An MSc conversion course in IT is popular amongst many graduates coming from non-IT disciplines for a number of reasons:

▌ It is a much more general IT course, combining technical and managerial topics.
▌ It will allow you to keep your IT career path open and flexible.
▌ Vendor-specific accreditation (such as Microsoft Certified Systems Engineer) can be achieved.
▌ It is a relatively short course (one year full-time)

Further information
For details of conversion courses see the Association of Graduate Careers Advisory Service (AGCAS) Survey: *Postgraduate Courses in Information Technology and Information Engineering* available from the careers service. Alternatively, contact your preferred university directly.

Writing a successful CV

Sooner or later, there will come a time when you need to respond to a job advertisement, not only by writing a letter of application, saying why you would like the job, but also by sending a current copy of your CV. A CV has just one main purpose – to get you an interview with your employer; in other words, it must sell you (and your skills) to the employer in about 20 seconds, because that is the average time spent reading one. Writing a CV (and keeping it up-to-date) is something you should take very seriously. It is often the only weapon you have in getting past the front door of many personnel departments. With this point in mind, I suggest you read the following book: *How To Write a CV,* published by Kogan Page.

How to write a top IT CV

Most, if not all, of the current IT publications have a section on careers, usually written by a panel of IT and recruitment experts. Similarly, many of the careers Web sites mentioned in Chapter 13 provide advice on interview technique and CV writing skills. If there is one piece of advice I can give you that expresses the opinions of many recruitment experts, it would be to warn you there is no such thing as the 'perfect' CV. Different IT employers prefer different styles of presentation in the CVs they are sent. Some experts for instance recommend putting all your technical skills on the last page of your CV. Other experts suggest that, if presented clearly, along with specific details of technical training courses attended, technical information stated on the first page of a CV will help employers identify your suitability for the position very quickly (remember the 20-second rule). Unfortunately, this is a decision that only you can make. Obviously, do not make it lightly, try and do some research about the company and its IT department first to get an idea of the role, and ultimately, the selection criteria that the company might adopt.

There is, however, some agreement amongst the majority of IT and recruitment professionals in some key areas of CV design and presentation. All suggest you should identify your business skills as well as your technical skills. Do not forget that most IT organisations no longer want IT 'nerds', they want professionals who can communicate equally well with IT and business people alike. Similarly, just because you have stated (as most people do on a CV) that '… I helped implement a new system called xyz on time and within budget', it doesn't tell the employer what you *actually* did, nor does it tell the employer what skills you used or gained during the project. Sell yourself by all means, but help a potential employer measure your abilities. Always try and relate your technical skills and tasks performed to actual (and even better, to *measurable*) business benefits. After each statement you make on your CV, always ask the question…so what? The answer should then form part of your original statement. You may be the world's greatest programmer, but you still need to convince a future employer that you are aware of how to utilise your technical skills to instigate change and deliver benefits to the business as a result (either by increasing profits or reducing costs). A bit of humility costs nothing.

Top CV tips

▍ Don't send the same 'standard' CV for every job. Tailor it for each position you apply for.
▍ Don't mention salary expectations.
▍ Be brief – even if you have a lot of skills and experience.
▍ Do mention *relevant* skills and experience.
▍ Put the most relevant and impressive information on the first page – even if it is not the most recent.
▍ Personal details and school exam results will not turn heads – put them on the last page.
▍ Use marketing devices to sell yourself – but don't lie on your CV.
▍ Technical skills and training undertaken may help an employer assess your capabilities – it might also put them off if you don't mention business skills too.

▐ Where possible, express your contribution to the organisation in financial terms. If you helped the company save £2 million by developing a new application, say so.

Networking

In an industry obsessed with technology it is easy to forget that there is a human element within the IT profession; even in the most technologically advanced companies it is *people* who make key decisions – one of whom will be the person conducting your next job interview. With so many ways of differentiating between candidates with similar skills, such as track record, references and employment history, let alone more advanced techniques such as graphology and psychometric testing, it's worth remembering that interviewers are human (well most of them are at least). If you can make an effort to appeal to their 'human' side (assuming they have one), there is a good chance you can overcome some of the barriers preventing you from getting that top job in IT.

The phrase 'it's not what you know, it's who you know', is often brought up during many debates on career development and recruitment. We all know it's not particularly fair, but that's how it is, and in that respect, the IT industry is no different to any other. You might be wondering why this apparent 'favouritism' is an issue affecting an industry that complains of severe skills shortages practically every week in the popular IT publications. True, there is no substitute for technical skills, especially in such fundamental IT roles as programming and technical support, but that is only one part of the selection process for potential employees. The IT industry doesn't have the longest and cleanest pedigree in the world, and it is just as incestuous as any other when it comes to career networking and job-hopping. Unlike the early days of commercial computing in the 1950s, possessing binary as a second language will no longer guarantee you a top job in IT; more likely it will pave the way for a lengthy stay in a suitably-appointed rest home.

Today's IT industry is very much focused on business and unless you are a technical wizard who lives in a cave, you will need to manage relationships with other business professionals.

People skills are now as important as technical skills for many top employers. At worst, you might be able to use these skills later in your career as a manager or consultant; more optimistically, you may be able to improve your recruitment and promotion prospects if you know how to use your contacts within an organisation. This is where career networking comes into its own – setting out to meet and build a rapport with each and every person who can influence the outcome of your application and offer you that top job in IT. Career networking has been derided by many in the past, but in an industry such as IT, which is continually changing and reinventing itself, planning for the future has never been so important. IT employees, in particular, are renowned for moving jobs fairly frequently – you never know where you might end up, so it is important to build and maintain bridges, even if it is just a Christmas card once a year.

Of course, the easy way to start networking is by attending some of the many IT seminars and conferences held regularly throughout the year. The majority of them are fun and lively (but with a serious message) and you will find it relatively straightforward to have a chat with people and swap business cards (or e-mail addresses) whilst enjoying a nice glass of Chardonnay.

Joining a professional IT association, such as the British Computer Society (BCS), is also a good way of expanding your contacts whilst at the same time benefiting from the many career development services they offer. The BCS has come a long way in the last few years and is much more in tune with the rank and file IT professionals as well as the big industry and academic 'bigwigs'. At the time of writing, there were over 37,000 BCS members, with membership growing steadily each month. Never before has the BCS been so popular, especially amongst graduate and student members.

Matthew Jones

Matthew Jones has successfully changed career direction as a result of using his networking skills and using the services of a professional career advisory firm, Career Design International.

Originally, Matthew had a degree in engineering and worked in the textile industry as a manager after graduating, gaining useful skills in man management and planning. From there he moved to a small management consultancy firm that provided advice to the textile and clothing sectors. However, Matthew soon decided that the long-term prospects for the textile industry were not good and decided to change his career to improve them.

To realise his ambitions, Matthew decided to enrol on an MBA course at Aston University, completing modules in finance, marketing, organisational behaviour and operations. Luckily for Matthew, the University had links with Career Design International, which offered support for its postgraduates. Through the service, they polished Matthew's CV, improved his presentation and communication skills and introduced him to key people in a number of different industries. In addition, Matthew also consulted the Association of MBAs, which was happy to advise on possible careers and provide contacts through its alumni. Using this advice Matthew identified the IT sector as the best place for his talents and somewhere where he could achieve his career goals. Matthew took the plunge and enrolled on an IT project management course before attending local and national IT recruitment fairs, where he used his networking and communication skills to great effect.

Matthew is now an IT consultant working for a professional services company. He offers the following advice to others who might be in a similar position to the one he found himself in: 'Don't get despondent, be open and receptive to professional career advice. Use academic and industrial contacts and don't be ashamed about it.'

Top networking tips

▌ Try and attend as many IT conferences, seminars and social events as possible in the area in which you want to work. (Seminars and conference dates are published regularly in

Computer Weekly, as are British Computer Society dinners and evening presentations).

▌ Quickly identify who are the key players in that area; the decision *influencers* and the decision *makers*.

▌ Learn who these people trust and why.

▌ Discover who works closely with these trusted people – do you know any of them?

▌ Offer your unconditional help. Try and provide them with a one-page synopsis of a bright idea for their area.

Useful contacts

The Association of MBAs
15 Duncan Terrace
London N1 8BZ
Tel: (020) 7837 3375
Web site: www.mba.org.uk

The British Computer Society
1 Sanford Street
Swindon
Wiltshire SN1 1HJ
Tel: 01793 417417

The full BCS diary of events and application details can be found on its Web site: www.bcs.org.uk

Training

Training is often seen as a 'silver bullet' to many inexperienced job hunters, especially those outside the IT profession. Training will allow you to apply for all the best jobs – at a price of course. Professional training does not come cheap, nor does it come with any guarantees of success in a future career.

If your current skills are not sufficient to allow you to move into the IT profession, you have two options. If you have a good degree you could consider joining a large IT consultancy company where specific IT skills are not always required. Alternatively, you could obtain the skills you need by undertaking a training course (as some of the case studies have shown). If you are currently working in a non-IT role, but have a desire to move into a pure IT role within the same organisation, training can help. Successful organisations cannot afford to lose skilled and experienced staff. Discuss your career aspirations with your manager and state your case for training. Training is costly, but it is also a worthwhile investment in people, so you must identify how the course will benefit both the organisation and your career. In most cases, your organisation will look favourably on paying part or all of your tuition fees – it helps them reduce recruitment fees and helps tie you into the company for a bit longer.

The type and format of training required is largely dependent on what skills you need in the role you are considering. It is certainly true that more and more companies now value vendor-specific training as highly as academic qualifications; however, they do limit your career options.

Holding a good degree or postgraduate degree, such as an MSc or PhD will give you many of the 'people' skills you will need in the IT industry and, depending on your course, many of the IT skills too. This is good news for anyone wanting a top job in IT; many of the top IT software and professional services companies have their own (highly acclaimed) graduate entry and training programmes and fast-track career progression schemes for real 'high-fliers' (people like you, in other words).

If you are seeking a career move from another profession, training may well help fill in some of the gaps in your IT skills, especially in key skill areas such as Java, e-commerce and project management. The type of training people acquire is usually a good indication of the IT employment market. After all no one would want training in a technology that was falling out of favour. Table 12.1 should give you a good idea of some of the more popular training topics.

Microsoft skills training

There is no doubt that possessing Microsoft skills will enhance your career prospects and, in many cases, give you a greater earnings potential. A recent Microsoft survey identified average earnings for those people possessing Microsoft certification. The

Table 12.1 The top 10 training topics during 1999/2000

Rank	Course
1	NT 4.0 support/admin
2	Web site design/development
3	Windows 2000
4	Network basics
5	Unix
6	IT and project management
7	Microsoft SQL
8	Java
9	Visual Basic
10	TCP/IP

(Main sources: *Aris, Key Training, KnowledgePool, NETg, New Horizons, Tower Education*)

results of the survey appear in Figure 12.1. Do not be led into a false sense of security though. Achieving Microsoft certification is certainly useful – no one ever got the sack for choosing Microsoft products, but gaining experience in them is what matters. Make this your priority.

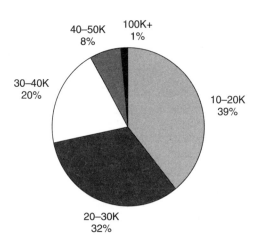

Figure 12.1 Average earnings for people possessing Microsoft certification

Key Microsoft certification programmes
Microsoft Certified Systems Engineer (MCSE)

The MCSE award is now considered a 'must-have' requirement for many IT organisations using Microsoft technology. The award is designed for IT professionals who analyse business requirements and design and implement a Microsoft-based solution, using products such as Windows 2000 and Microsoft server software. Typical IT roles that recruit MCSE-qualified staff include:

- systems engineers;
- technical support engineers;
- network analysts;
- technical consultants.

Microsoft Certified Professional (MCP)

The MCP award is for people who have the skills to successfully implement a Microsoft product or technology within an organisation. Hands-on skills are a requirement for this award.

Microsoft Certified Solution Developer (MCSD)

The MCSD award is designed for professionals who design and develop leading-edge solutions using Microsoft development tools, technologies and platforms, and the Windows DNA architecture. An MCSD will be able to develop desktop applications as well as multi-user Web-based and transaction-based applications. A feature of the exam will test the candidate's ability to build Web-based applications using Microsoft's application server and other products such as SQL server and Visual Studio. Typical IT roles that recruit MCSE-qualified staff include:

- systems engineers;
- technical support engineers;
- network analysts;
- technical consultants.

How to obtain Microsoft training

Microsoft's authorised training partners are known as certified technical education centres (CTECs). Using these training providers will help you obtain all the popular Microsoft qualifications, including the much in demand Windows 2000 administrator courses. There

171

are, however, courses from Microsoft partners such as SmartForce and NETg, and as non-CTECs (as are the well-established Learning Tree training group) they have more freedom to depart from the official curriculum. Such independence is seen as a benefit within many IT organisations as these companies will give you the 'warts and all' story, taking into account the fact that Microsoft products have to coexist with products from other suppliers.

Official Microsoft training
For further details on CTECs, visit Microsoft's Web site: www.microsoft.com/train-cert/providers or call (0800) 973031. This site gives details of instructor-led classroom courses, online courses with access to trainers and self-study courses for those of you who are confident enough to work without the aid of a safety net.

Independent Microsoft training centres:

SmartForce Tel: (020) 8282 1800
Learning Tree Tel: (01372) 364600
New Horizon Tel: (020) 7684 2000
NETg Tel: (020) 8994 4404
QA Training Tel: (01285) 640181

Java skills training

There are two levels of Java certification – Sun Certified Java Programmer and Sun Certified Java Developer. To gain the developer certificate you must first pass the certified programmer exam. The Java programming language course offered by Sun is a five-day workshop leading to Java programmer certification and costs £1,250.

There are plenty of other sources of generalised Java training, or you can approach trainers attached to the suppliers whose Java development environments you will be using, such as Microsoft's Visual J++ and Jscript, Netscape's Javascript, IBM's VisualAge or Symantec's Visual Café.

Further information
Sun Microsystems
Tel: (01276) 416520 or www.sun.co.uk/suned

Network skills training

Novell and Microsoft both offer qualifications in networking, as does Cisco. Cisco training is available from GeoTrain. Novell has a network of authorised education centres such as IT-IQ and Xpertise Training in the UK, which offer training on all Novell products and certification courses such as Certified Novell Engineer (CNE) and Certified Novell Administrator (CNA). Other network trainers include: Tech Connect and The Knowledge Centre (part of QA Training).

Further information

Xpertise Training Tel: (0345) 573888 or www.xpertise-training.com

IT-IQ Tel: (020) 7670 3300 or www.it-iq.co.uk

GeoTrain Tel: (01628) 594700 or www.geotrain.com

Tech Connect Tel: (020) 8549 0549 or www.tech-connect.com

The Knowledge Centre Tel: (01252) 715155 or www.qa.com

General IT skills training

There is a multitude of hardware and software vendors, as well as independent training organisations that provide a wide range of IT training courses. However, the Information Systems Examination Board (ISEB), affiliated to the British Computer Society, is widely considered by many IT employees and employers to be one of the best training organisations within the UK. To date the ISEB has awarded over 60,000 qualifications in the following subjects:

- project management;
- service management;
- business and management skills;
- SSADM4+;
- software analysis and design;
- software testing;
- information security.

Further information

Information on the ISEB and the full range of ISEB certified examination topics can be obtained from:

Customer Services
The British Computer Society
1 Sanford Street
Swindon
Wiltshire SN1 1HJ
Or by telephoning: (01793) 417417

Consultancy skills training

An independent qualification in consultancy is being worked on and will be overseen by the BCS ISEB. Topics will be covered in three training sessions, each lasting three days, and will include:

Session 1: meeting clients, research, structured interviewing, planning and structuring an assignment, identifying the requirement, preparing proposals, building and maintaining relationships, making recommendations and planning for disengagement;

Session 2: consulting tools and techniques, interviewing skills, facilitation skills, solving problems and making decisions, writing reports, project management essentials, team working and managing client expectations;

Session 3: managing consultancy, building long-term relationships, understanding organisations, managing change, selling consultancy services and bidding for contracts, managing a consultancy team and principles of managing a consultancy practice.

IT management skills training

It is important to remember that there is (thankfully) more to life in the IT profession than just programming. Many people considering a rewarding career in IT have considerable business and management experience or highly sought after postgraduate qualifications such as an MBA. If you possess these types of skills and qualifications, you should consider gaining specific IT management (and project management) skills to help you transfer your career to one focused on IT.

The Cranfield School of Management (part of Cranfield University) is widely recognised as providing courses aimed at IT managers and executives. Its courses range from one day to five days and cover topics such as IT project management, consultancy skills and e-business and managing information systems.

Further information
Full course schedules and information can be obtained from:

Cranfield School of Management
Cranfield
Bedford MK43 0AL
Tel: (01234) 751122
or visit their Web site: www.cranfield.ac.uk

Internet security skills training

Internet security training is available from many IT training organisations that advertise in _Computing_ and _Computer Weekly_, including for example, QA Training (Tel: (01285) 655888) and NetConnect (Tel: (020) 7573 5100). Other training courses are run by many of the major suppliers of security hardware and software (eg firewalls), such as Checkpoint and virus protection companies such as Network Associates and Sophos. All these companies have further details on their respective Web sites: www.checkpoint.com; www.networkassociates.com and www.sophos.com.

Paul

At the beginning of the year Paul was in charge of 14 police constables, now he works as a technical support analyst for a leading UK company. Whilst working for the police, Paul, who has a degree in Law, began to gain an interest in IT, and becoming more and more frustrated with his own career development, decided to investigate a possible career move into the IT profession. As a first step, he paid to study for the

---

A+ PC technician exam with an independent training company. The course taught him how to build a PC, which he thought would provide him with some good basic problem-solving skills. At about the same time, Paul also enrolled for an MSc in IT for Management and, for good measure, applied and was granted membership of the British Computer Society. He decision to opt for an MSc was based on the fact that Paul had no real experience of IT, and realising many employers wanted at least six months' experience, thought it would help his case.

Paul was initially convinced that he would have to complete his MSc before an employer would take him seriously. Not so. After seeing an advert in *Computer Weekly*, Paul sent his details to a well-known IT services company that was looking for people with any type of customer service experience. No IT experience was required. At the interview, the support manager for the company was impressed with Paul's customer-facing skills. He was not concerned about his IT skills – these can be taught, people skills are another matter altogether – you either have them or you don't.

Paul was offered the job, and has since been sent on a number of training courses paid for by his employer to gain helpdesk skills. In addition, they have also sent Paul on a Prince2 project management course and helped him pass the Certified Cisco Network Administrator (CCNA) exam.

13 *Where to find top IT jobs*

Planning your IT career

This book can help you find and prepare you for a top job in IT, but it cannot guarantee that you will be offered the first job you apply for. Even though there is currently a severe skills shortage affecting the IT industry, this is no guarantee that the skills you possess are those required by an employer. To be successful in achieving your career aims, you must plan every stage of the way. The following questions should give you a few ideas on how to plan your IT career:

1. Does the idea of contracting appeal to you – or do you prefer the relative security of permanent employment?
2. In what area of IT would you like to work (software, consultancy, hardware, multimedia, telecommunications, e-commerce)?
3. What skills do you need to work in the IT area you chose in Question 2?
4. What skills do you possess – are they in demand or nearly obsolete?
5. What job role suits your current skills best?
6. Where do you want to be in five years' time?
7. Do you know what skills you will need to achieve your longer term career aspirations?
8. Can you join a graduate training programme or a programme for experienced professionals?
9. Where would you like to work? (Locally, anywhere in the UK, anywhere in the world?)
10. Where are you *able* to work (are you mobile, or must you work near where you live?)

Armed with this information, you can now decide how to make your first move to help you get you a job in IT. You could decide to defer writing job applications until you have gained specific skills or training, as mentioned later in the book, or you could decide to enter the industry straight away.

Finding a top IT job

There are a number of sources you can use to help find a job within the IT profession. Figure 13.1 shows the main sources of information for IT job hunters, but it is not a definitive list – you must also act on your own initiative. It is said that many IT jobs are never advertised. Why? Well, the main reason is because word has got around about the vacancy and it has been filled on the basis of personal recommendation, or by someone 'being in the right place at the right time'. Unfortunately, the IT industry is no different from any other in that sense. Whatever job you do apply for, you can be sure of one thing – many others will be applying for it too, so anything you can do to help swing things in your favour will be a worthwhile effort. Chapter 12, 'Getting in and getting on', will help you to think more about the things you can do to enhance your job-seeking prospects.

Local newspapers

Many local and national newspapers advertise vacancies for computing and IT staff, usually under the heading 'Professional' or 'Technical Appointments'. If you have restricted your job-search area to a regional area, then you will have a much better chance of finding a suitable job if you read your local papers regularly. Before you rush out and buy a copy, check which day the IT jobs are advertised. Many larger regional papers tend to have a specific day for certain types of job vacancies. For instance, the *Manchester Evening News* advertises computing and IT vacancies on a Tuesday.

National newspapers

Whilst the national daily newspapers generally advertise more computing and IT jobs than their local counterparts, these jobs are

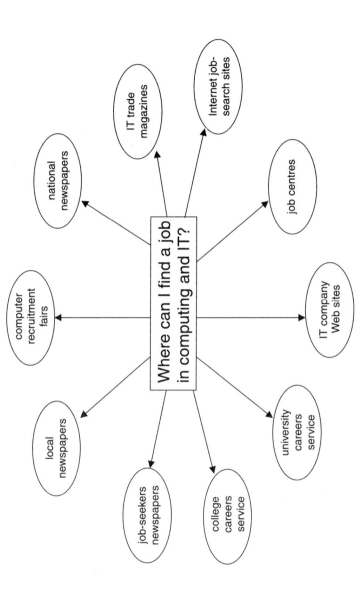

Figure 13.1 The main sources of information for IT job-hunters

primarily aimed at graduates and those IT professionals seeking a more senior role. As you would expect, national newspapers advertise national computing and IT vacancies to be found all over the UK, and in many cases they advertise jobs in other countries too; Table 13.1 provides details of which national newspapers to read and when to read them.

Specialist 'job-seekers' newspapers

Often published weekly, these large-format newspapers are full of jobs and careers advice, usually for a particular region of the UK (*Yorkshire Jobs*, for instance). Whilst general in nature, catering for many different professions, they are categorised quite well. IT jobs appear under headings such as 'Technical', 'Professional' or 'Computing'.

IT trade magazines

With an industry diverse as IT, is it not a complete surprise to find a large number of both general and specialist magazines published specifically for the IT professional. Not all of these, however, include appointments sections, but it is worth paying a visit to the library to have a read of them all the same. The main two magazines that contain advertisements (as well as lots of other useful information, technical articles and news) are *Computing* and *Computer Weekly*. Both are well established and pride themselves on the staggering number of IT vacancies they publish. They are free to people working in the IT industry, or you can buy them at most newsagents or read them at most libraries.

Table 13.1 Where to find IT jobs in national newspapers

Newspaper	Advertises IT jobs on
The Guardian	Thursday
The Daily Telegraph	Thursday, Saturday
The Sunday Telegraph	Sunday
The Times	Thursday
The Sunday Times	Sunday

General computing and IT publications
Computing
VNU Business Publications
VNU House
32–34 Broadwick Street
London W1A 2HG
Tel: (020) 8842 0008
Free subscription Web site: www.vnusubs.co.uk
Publication Web site: www.computing.co.uk

Computer Weekly
Reed Business Publishing
Quadrant House
The Quadrant
Sutton
Surrey SM2 5AS
Tel: (01444) 441212
Web site: www.computerweekly.co.uk

Networking and telecommunications publications
Network News
VNU Business Publications
VNU House
32–34 Broadwick Street
London W1A 2HG
Tel: (020) 8842 0008
Web site: www.networknews.co.uk

Network Week
CMP House
8–14 Vine Hill
London EC1R 5AXC
Tel: (020) 8845 8545

IT consultancy publications
Management Consultancy
VNU Business Publications
VNU House
32–34 Broadwick Street
London W1A 2HG
Tel: (020) 8842 0008
Web site: www.vnusubs.co.uk/managementconsultancy

General interest magazines
Internet Business
Haymarket Management Publications Ltd
174 Hammersmith Road
London W6 7JP
Tel: (020) 8267 4625
Web site: www.ibmag.co.uk

PC Home, PC Advisor, Windows Expert, PC Basics
IDG Media
Media House
Adlington Park
Macclesfield
Cheshire SK10 4NP
Tel: (01625) 87888

Accessing job vacancies from the Internet

There are numerous recruitment Web sites you can use in your search for a top job in IT. Some are specifically for graduates, some cater for professionals with at least one year's experience. Table 13.2 identifies some of the more popular ones. In addition, you can read hundreds of helpful articles on the latest technologies, issues and general career advice.

I doubt whether there is any major employer that doesn't have its own Web site. With the Internet now becoming one of the most popular methods of communication, many companies now prefer to provide all their corporate details on their Web site, including recruitment details. In fact, many large organisations have now dismissed traditional paper-based methods of recruitment altogether, preferring to recruit staff online. In general, online

Table 13.2 Useful Web sites for IT vacancies

Web Site Address	Focus	Area	E-mail Vacancies
www.haymarket.co.uk	Professional	UK	✓
www.graduateconnection.ac.uk	Graduate	Midlands	✓
www.careers.ncl.ac.uk/NEGD	Graduate	North-East	✓
http://cchp2.swan.ac.uk	Graduate	Wales	
www.topjobs.net	Professional	UK	✓
www.topgrad.net	Graduate	UK	✓
www.stepstone.co.uk	Graduate/ Professional	UK	✓
www.computerweekly.com	Graduate/ Professional	UK	✓
www.jobclub.co.uk	Professional	UK	
www.jobworld.co.uk	Professional	UK	✓
www.jobserve.co.uk	Professional	UK	✓
www.ragtime.co.uk	(Under)graduate placement/ vacation	UK	✓

applications make it easier for the recruiter and employers to store and share CVs with other interested parties. However, for most senior posts, traditional methods of recruitment are still preferred – well, in the short-term at least. Goldjobs (www.goldjobs.com) is a new online recruitment site, which will only offer IT and telecoms jobs that pay £100,000 a year or more. Goldjobs will offer the talented (as well as the envious) the chance to view jobs with only a minimal number of mouse clicks (four) and will protect their anonymity until they decide to declare it during the selection process. If this is more your idea of a top job, then what are you waiting for? Good luck, and if you are offered a £100K a year job, remember where you read about it first.

The pros and cons of online job hunting

The greatest advantage the Internet provides over more traditional forms of job hunting is speed. In theory at least, agencies can e-mail you with the latest job vacancies as soon as they are created and usually well before they appear in the usual recruitment magazines.

Equally, the ease of applying over the Internet means that you can register with a few agencies at the same time with little effort, sending an electronic copy of your CV to each one. I stress the word *few*. Whilst you may be tempted to register with as many agencies as possible, you will soon find that you lose control over the situation. It is much more sensible to get to know the agency you are dealing with and for them to understand your needs.

Opinion on which agencies to use varies. One marketing manager at a top IT recruitment agency recommends starting with Jobserve, Computerweekly.com, Jobworld, Stepstone plus your favourite recruitment agency. Others, however, suggest starting off with names you know from the offline world of recruitment (such as Rullion and Computer People), which have a reputation to protect. That way you are less likely to fall prey to Web site operators who have little or no knowledge of the IT job market. Some of the better agencies will only alert you to suitable jobs based on your profile (which you complete online), saving you the time and hassle of sifting through hundreds of potential jobs.

Top tips for online job applications

▌ Use a common format for your CV, such as Microsoft Word.
▌ Your application should be formal, attractive and clear in its presentation.
▌ Ensure the content of your application is relevant to the post you are applying for.
▌ Think carefully before sending 'gimmicky' CVs (such as those incorporating photos or audio and video clips). They may be used (albeit unconsciously) to discriminate between applicants when sifting through forms rather than when talking to people in an interview.

Cybercafés

Cybercafés are becoming quite popular places for young and trendy IT professionals to meet and have a strong dose of Java (the coffee bean, not the language). Many of them can be found on the high street in major cities, but supermarkets such as Tesco now provide Internet access within their cafés in some of their larger stores. Most cybercafés charge hourly for access, with discounts for registering as a member and off-peak usage.

Virtual chat rooms

Virtual chat rooms are either e-mail sites or Web-based forums that allow people with a common interest to communicate with each other. When they first appeared, they tended to be thought of as places that only the sad, the serious or the lonely frequented; now they are stimulating and vibrant and provide a fertile recruiting ground for some of the largest IT employers. Employers desperate to recruit top skills in a very short timescale are slowly reaching the conclusion that the best place to find some of the best technical staff is within these chat rooms where people answer and discuss technical issues on a regular basis. As one of the new 'e-head-hunters' has commented, 'the most likely place to find someone with Java skills is a Java chat room'. BT is already using virtual chat rooms as a means of headhunting potential recruits by using special software that seeks out appropriate chat groups on the Internet. Some other employers 'lurk' in online discussion groups to find potential employees, but in all cases, employers will follow up their top 'catches' with an e-mail and then a formal interview.

During a six-week trial of 'chat-room' recruitment, BT interviewed four people, but did not take them on because they lacked the business skills the company wanted. BT, whilst realising that technical forums were not the best place to find business candidates, still intend to use the technique to search for software developers – in particular Web and mobile phone software developers.

Registering with an IT recruitment agency

The current skills shortage in the IT profession is generating huge amounts of work for the specialist IT recruitment agencies, whose main objective is to match their registered clients with vacancies from the IT companies they help. Whilst the majority of IT companies will have a personnel department, they will often use recruitment agencies to advertise vacancies and perform selection interviews on their behalf, because they do not have the time to handle the hundreds of (often unsuitable) applications they would otherwise receive. Agencies are very popular with many IT professionals as they are extremely good at getting them a large number of interviews in a relatively short space of time. Agencies work on a commission basis, receiving payment from the recruiting company usually for every candidate sent for interview plus a bonus payment should they accept the position (usually a percentage of their starting salary).

You may be wondering why I am even bothering to tell you how agencies earn a living – unfortunately it is quite important. There can be problems using recruitment agencies. Whilst they will bend over backwards to find you work if you possess real skills and experience in key areas, they will soon lose interest in you if you cannot offer them the skills they are seeking. Many of these agencies employ highly skilled, sincere professionals, who will gladly offer career advice and guidance – but they are not a charity. Nevertheless, because of the skills shortage, many agencies are now looking for IT graduates straight from university as well as experienced professionals (minimum six months' experience is expected from many agencies – work undertaken during a 'sandwich' or 'gap' year will do). Lists of specialist computer recruitment agencies can be found in *Computing* and *Computer Weekly* or find them in the *Yellow Pages*, listed under 'Employment Agencies'.

Approaching employers directly

Whilst it is all very good taking the initiative and contacting employers directly, studies have suggested this is really not worth doing unless you have 'inside knowledge' of a vacancy that has not yet been advertised or know someone within the organisation who will help with your application.

In one study, over 80 per cent of 'test' applicants who applied directly to the employer were politely informed that 'there were no vacancies at the present time, but your details would be kept on file'. When the employers were asked three months later about the application details filed, they admitted they did not really have time to sift through any of the applications in the file, apart from those received in response to a specific advertisement.

If you are confident you _can_ bypass the normal recruitment process, then write a short, simple letter to the IT recruitment manager (or Personnel Manager), explaining your skills and interests, preferably enclosing a copy of your CV. If possible, find out the name of this manager and address your letter accordingly – it will usually guarantee someone will at least read it. The following points are worth heeding when writing a speculative letter to an employer for any IT vacancy:

▌ Type your letter (or use a word-processor) on good quality white A4 paper.
▌ Briefly describe your skills and experience in one paragraph (the rest is on your CV).
▌ State your availability for an informal discussion or interview should they be interested.
▌ Leave a contact address and phone number.
▌ Always enclose an SAE for their reply.

Further information

Details of IT companies, including contact addresses and the software and hardware they use, can be found in _The Computer Users Year Book_, usually available from the reference section of most libraries.

Key employers

There are literally hundreds of employers who are seeking people with IT skills throughout the UK; the majority of IT jobs in the UK, however, are still to be found in South-East England. Figure 13.2 will give you an idea of how the majority of IT companies are distributed throughout the UK and Eire.

Whilst it is good practice to read the IT trade magazines mentioned within this chapter for names of IT companies and agencies, many people like to know the names of at least a few of the larger organisations when they are thinking about applying for a job. To get you started, here is a list of some of the leading IT employers in the UK. A brief introductory letter or telephone call to any one of these may help you get started; all the following

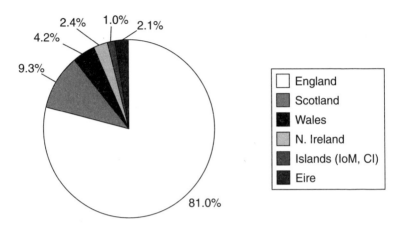

Figure 13.2   The distribution of IT companies within the UK and Eire

companies participate in the British Computer Society's Professional Development Scheme:

Avesta Sheffield Ltd

The BOC Group

Britannia Building Society

British Gas Transco

British Nuclear Fuels Ltd – IT Services

BT Networks and Systems

Cap Gemini Ernst & Young

Charles Schwab Europe

Cornwall District Council

Defence Research Agency

Essex County Council

Ford Motor Company

HM Land Registry

ICL

Lloyd's Register

London Borough of Camden

Manchester Metropolitan University

National Power plc

NATS Software Services

Oxford Radcliffe Hospital

PA Consulting Group

Post Office IT Services

Reuters Ltd

Royal & Sun Alliance

The Scottish Executive

South-East London Health

University of Wales Swansea

Vodafone Group plc

Which?

Employers in Northern Ireland

Despite the majority of IT sites being within England, there are a great many IT companies that are located in Northern Ireland, many of whom are large international software and services companies. _The Computer Users Year Book_ (_IT Sites_ supplement), available from main libraries, will provide information on IT sites throughout the UK and Eire. Alternatively, details of hardware, software and IT consultancy companies based in Northern Ireland can be found on the Web site: www.guide-to-nireland.com.

A few of the larger companies worth investigating include:

BIC Systems Ltd

Bull Information Systems

CFM Systems

Computastore

Coopers & Lybrand

Data General Ltd

Digital Equipment Company Ltd

How Systems Ltd

IBM (UK) Ltd

ICL (UK) Ltd

KPMG Peat Marwick

Lagan Technologies Ltd

McDonnell Information Systems (MDIS)

Nezz Networking

Nortel (Northern Telecom)

Parity Solutions (Ireland) Ltd

Real Time Systems Ltd

Siemens Nixdorf Information Systems

Vision Information Consulting

Zaray Internet Consultants

14 Useful addresses

The British Computer Society (BCS)
1 Sanford Street
Swindon
Wiltshire SN1 1HJ
Tel: (01793) 417417

The Council of European Professional Informatics Societies (CEPIS)
7 Mansfield Mews
London W1M 9FJ
Tel: (020) 7637 5607

The Engineering Council
10 Maltravers Street
London WC2R 3ER
Tel: (020) 7240 7891

The Institute of Data Processing Management (IDPM)
IDPM House
Edgington Way
Ruxley Corner
Sidcup
Kent DA14 5HR
Tel: (020) 8308 0747

15 *Further reading*

Job hunting

Bryon, M (1994) *How To Pass Graduate Recruitment Tests*, Kogan Page, London

Corfield, R (1999) *Successful Interview Skills*, 2nd edn, Kogan Page, London

Krechowiecka, I (2000) *Net That Job!*, 2nd edn, Kogan Page, London

Modha, S (1994) *How To Pass Computer Selection Tests*, Kogan Page, London

Education and qualifications

Sponsorship for Students

Published and distributed by the Careers Research Advisory Centre (CRAC) and Hobsons Publishing plc. Contains 2,500 scholarships and bursaries from 200 different organisations. Copies are available from Customer Services REF F30, Biblios PDS Ltd, Star Road, Partridge Green, West Sussex RH13 8LD. Tel: (01403) 710851.

Working abroad

Golzen, G & Kogan, H (2000) *The Daily Telegraph Guide to Working Abroad*, 22nd edn, Kogan Page, London

Useful books on IT

E-commerce

Fuller, F (2000) *Getting Started with Electronic Commerce*, The Dryden Press, Orlando, USA

Korper, S and Ellis, J (2000) *The E-Commerce Book: Building the E-Empire*, Academic Press, London

Kienan, B (2000) _Small Business Solutions for E-Commerce_, Microsoft Press, Washington, USA

Nokes, S (2000) _Startup.com: Everything you need to know about starting up an Internet company_, Financial Times/Prentice-Hall, London

Game design
De Goes, J (1999) _3D Game Programming with C++_, Coriolis Group Books, Arizona, USA

Saltzman, M (1999) _Game Design: Secrets of the Sages_, Brady Publishing, London

Networking
Derfler, F and Free, L (1998) _How Networks Work_, Que, Indianapolis, USA

Nance, B (1997) _Introduction to Networking_, Que, Indianapolis, USA

Systems development methodologies
Weaver, P L (1998) _Practical SSADM Version 4_, Financial Times Management, London

IT training material

Many libraries now stock computer training videos, covering subjects such as Microsoft Office, UNIX and Visual Basic.

A huge selection of computer manuals, computer-based training packages, CD ROMS and videos is available from most Internet bookshops (such as www.amazon.co.uk) or alternatively from:

Computer Manuals Ltd
28 Lincoln Road
Olton
Birmingham B27 6PA
Tel: (0121) 706 6000
Web site: www.computer-manuals.co.uk

Index

References in *italic* indicate figures or tables